FUTURE PROOF

ADVANCE PRAISE

"Future Proof is a great read for corporate executives looking to reinvent themselves in an ever more entrepreneurial economy."

—DORIE CLARK, AUTHOR OF *ENTREPRENEURIAL YOU, REINVENTING YOU AND STAND OUT*

"Diana's ability to see what senior leaders need to navigate the future of work is unparalleled."

—DONNA EIBY, FUTURE WORK SKILLS ACADEMY

"It is both a curse and a blessing of our fraught times that reinvention is no longer an option, but an obligation. Resilience rather than any formal qualification has become the key to both success and satisfaction. For those of us who would welcome a guide, I cannot recommend Future Proof too strongly."

—HENNY SENDER, *FINANCIAL TIMES*

"Sometimes it takes a tragedy to create the conditions for a new mindset and way of living. A challenge that emerges is to honour the loss of a loved one and to make what happens next bigger and better than what might have been before. Diana has discovered a playbook for how to be resilient from both a personal and professional perspective—the same approach will future proof your life and career."

—PETER WILLIAMS, CITIBANK, RESOLVE FOUNDATION, MUSIC FOR LIFE INTERNATIONAL

"There are many paths to a successful career. In Future Proof: Reinventing Work in an Age of Acceleration, Diana shows us how a long work life can yield many paths to impact and fulfillment."

—WILLARD MCCLOUD III, GLOBAL HEAD, DIVERSITY & INCLUSION AND CULTURE, PFIZER

"Future Proof is an important contribution to the Leadership section of bookstores as Diana is a master at getting leaders to step back, reflect, and make positive changes."

—STEVE DEKREY, ASSOCIATE DEAN, FOUNDING DIRECTOR, KELLOGG-HKUST EMBA PROGRAM; CHAIRMAN, INTERNATIONAL ACADEMIC COUNCIL, MOSCOW SCHOOL OF MANAGEMENT SKOLKOVO

"This book is not just for executives—this book is for everyone from college grads to your grandparents. We all need to reinvent ourselves constantly in an era of disruption, globalization, shifting trends, and new opportunities. Build on your strengths and find awesome new ways to succeed."

—ANGIE LAU, EX-BLOOMBERG TV ANCHOR, FOUNDER OF NARRAMUR AND FORKAST NEWS

"The ones at the top today run the biggest risk of extinction tomorrow due to hubris and blind spots to their self-awareness. In essence, what got many senior leaders to the upper rungs of their ladders most certainly won't get take them into the future. Future Proof is the mindset shift that corporate executives today need to be leaders of tomorrow."

—GULNAR VASWANI, CHIEF CULTURE OFFICER, LEADERSHIP RE-IMAGINED

"Diana has created a must-read book for leaders considering what skills they will need to future proof not only their organizations but their own sense of meaning in an age of disruption and acceleration."

—LALE KASEBI, FOUNDER & CEO, HUMAN-AT.WORK

"Everyone should read Future Proof, a real life guide to navigate, reinvent and measure their futures in the fast-changing world of the fourth industrial revolution."

—CLIVE LEE, CEO, YIDAN PRIZE

FUTURE PROOF

REINVENTING WORK IN THE AGE OF ACCELERATION

DIANA WU DAVID

FUTURE PROOF
Reinventing Work in the Age of Acceleration

ISBN 978-1-5445-1360-7 *Paperback*
978-1-5445-1359-1 *Ebook*

For Alan Wu, without whom none of this journey would be possible.

CONTENTS

future-proof

adjective

1. (of a product or system) unlikely to become obsolete.

verb

1. make (a product or system) future-proof.
2. "this approach allows you to future-proof your applications"

The concept of future-proofing is the process of anticipating the future and developing methods of minimizing the effects of shocks and stresses of future events. This term is commonly found in electronics, data storage, and communications systems.[1]

1 Oxford Dictionaries, *English Oxford Living Dictionaries*, accessed September 16, 2018, https://en.oxforddictionaries.com/definition/future-proof.

INTRODUCTION

How do we stay relevant in this ever-changing landscape? How do we spot upcoming trends that might affect us before we are in the crosshairs of obsolescence and disruption? How do we brand ourselves outside of a corporate role to sustain a contribution on our own terms? How can we find a tribe of our own away from the corporate watercooler? How can we measure our progress without annual budgets and performance reviews?

We're worried. We don't have time. We don't have bandwidth to answer all those calls and messages, not even the one from our doctor who will tell us to lay off the stress and long hours sitting at a desk or on a plane or in a conference room.

We like our work or are at *least* proud of what we've built—the skills and credibility. We have a lifestyle we enjoy. We are near the top of the mountain, if not at the summit. And yet, what have we sacrificed? Family? Health? Dreams of making a difference in the world? It seems like a pyrrhic victory, a string of carcasses strewn behind us that negate the true sense of achievement we were hoping to feel.

But people are talking about a hundred-year life. What could we do if we weren't doing this job? Who would want to talk to us once that director or doctor or partner title wasn't on our LinkedIn profile or business card?

Where would we start in planning for the future? We don't want to look silly. We don't want to seem ungrateful for all that we have and all that we've been given. But we're also scared shitless that if we don't do anything it will leave us vulnerable, our careers at the mercy of the company's board or disruptions in industry over time.

In writing this book, I'm making a few assumptions. Like, you have enough financial or career capital to take some risks, even if it means skipping your regular cappuccino. I take for granted that making a meaningful contribution and intellectual stimulation is important; that it would feel great to know you could quit or keep your job, on *your* terms; that taking a sabbatical, a day, or a week off to get your mojo back—or move to paradise full-time for that matter—would be an improvement on the status quo. I am assuming it would give you a deep sense of purpose to know you were making more of a difference again.

If the idea of work and life on your terms brings a sigh of wistfulness, you're not alone. You can wake up excited for the work ahead. The world needs you being creative, innovative, solving problems, building and investing in companies, connecting people, and mentoring the next generation.

You are not obsolete, but you may need to upgrade your operating system to future-proof your career and contributions to create more meaning, joy, and purpose in your life.

Let's go.

WHY I WROTE THIS BOOK

I'd known my best friend Charlotte's husband for fifteen years. He wasn't the social type. I was puzzled when the phone rang in my Hong Kong office and I heard George's voice. He *never* called me.

Pressing the phone to my ear, I heard his familiar, steady voice. "Diana, I need to tell you about Charlotte."

His voice wavered. "She...she killed herself last night."

I went cold. Dumbstruck, I felt the blood drain from me.

"What? Why? How did it happen?" I asked, and again, "*Why*?"

I stared at the computer monitor, seeing nothing. Row after row of emails blurred into a gray, unimportant, and trivial mass. My hands went cold and seemed like they belonged to someone else as they grasped the phone. Panting and dizzy with confusion and heartbreak, I could feel my mind grasping for something to do to keep the world from spinning out of control, but suddenly everything about my neat little office at *Financial Times* seemed alien.

The door creaked open. "Diana, we have a conference call in fifteen. Everything all right?"

"Yes, I'm fine. Just need a moment."

People speak about pivotal moments that serve as a wake-up call, an invitation to stop living on autopilot. Charlotte's death made me realize the shortness of life and the futility of making do. When I looked around, I saw many other people feeling the same way. The senior people in the board director programs I had launched at *Financial Times* were looking out at the next twenty, thirty, or forty years of increasing longevity and wondering what their role would be as an elder in the business community. With the pace of change accelerating, technology rendering their knowledge obsolete, and a globally competitive landscape, few can rely on a nice pension and guaranteed well-paid corporate board position at retirement. At the top of their game they were peering over a cliff wondering what the stepping stone might be to a new life that allows them to re-balance and invest in the hobbies, relationships, and interests that were sacrificed to get to the top. The good news is that the life of narrow reliance on one specialty is a risk that can be lessened by investing in a wider realm of activities and a broader network of relationships.

Around the same time as Charlotte's untimely death, TEDx was auditioning speakers for an event on the theme of "crossroads." A friend encouraged me to try out, and I signed up for the audition. What did I have to say about crossroads? I wasn't even sure, but this was an opportunity to practice storytelling, and that was part of becoming a better writer, which I aspired to be. I thought I'd probably fall flat on my face, but that was okay because I was putting myself out there, and I was trying.

I don't know what I expected, but I told myself that if I could help just one person, it would all be worth it.

Unlike in past years, the decision was not up to the judges

but to the several hundred people who they had invited for the TEDx open mic. Each table had a rating sheet for the speakers. As I approached the microphone on stage, I was terrified, but I started talking, and the more I talked, the more relaxed I became. I told them about my friend Charlotte and how we were going to start our own consulting company and take over the world. I told them about how we had both done pretty well for ourselves, but somewhere along the way, we had abandoned our dreams and settled for being the women other people expected us to be. I told them about losing Charlotte and how that had driven me to a crossroads in my own life. I could stay on the path of least resistance, or I could be brave and strive to build a life that made my heart sing.

After my talk, a woman approached me at the bar. "I really needed to hear that right now," she said. We talked for a while, and I knew then that I had helped at least one person.

I was chosen to speak at the upcoming TEDx Stage Event.

I spent a long time writing my speech. It needed to be real and raw and authentic, but I worried that I might be committing career suicide. One of my friends who read the speech laughed and said that it looked like I was going to live out my midlife crisis onstage. Was it trivial and narcissistic? Was I crazy to share such a personal story?

Would it be just passing gossip to people? I wrote more and practiced more and then went to rehearse my speech for the TEDx organizers. One, a computer science professor, said he could completely relate and asked me to make it more relatable to both women *and* men. A television anchor was fascinated and asked for more visceral detail. They actually wanted to listen and could see how it fit into their own lives. It was more than just my story. I had learned something important that other people needed to hear. I had something to share.

The TEDx was held at the Hong Kong Performing Arts Center. There were two thousand people in attendance. The masters of ceremony were Angie Lau, a charismatic Bloomberg TV anchor, and Jesko von den Steinen, an actor, choreographer, and filmmaker. They even had Cirque de Soleil dancers at intermission. I was way out of my league.

I spoke and was overwhelmed by the response. People came up to me afterward to share their stories. Not just people in their forties and fifties but young people who told me they had great but unfulfilling careers and they didn't know what to do. I had tapped into a fear—and a void—that people across generations were experiencing.

What I expressed that had resonated with these people is our need to give ourselves permission to live life on our own terms. This means pursuing our work within the context of our lives instead of living our lives around the edges of our work. It also means learning how to navigate a workplace where the traditional metrics of success are giving way to priorities of well-being and wisdom, influenced by millennials interested in meaning and boomers prioritizing growth and continued engagement into later years. It is fundamentally about being ambitious to live the life we imagine, not the one we've been given.

Afterwards, people continued contacting me. They wanted to talk about what was going on in their lives. I wanted to know what was working for others and to share it, so I started writing. This book is about that journey and those stories—what I found and what you have the opportunity to discover if you give yourself permission to invest in life.

I've spoken on this topic at numerous companies, from Credit Suisse to Expedia to Li & Fung. This desire to live life on one's own terms and the failure to do so is not an isolated or unusual experience; it is part of the zeitgeist of today's corporate world, and we see its manifestation in burnout and uncertainty.

Younger people are questioning where they are going. Middle-aged workers question where they currently are and how their lives might play out on that path. Older generations are looking to the future. Senior leaders want to keep working but are ready to make a change, too, thinking about a more meaningful second act.

Disruption, technology, AI, and robots in the workplace are going from the factory floor to the board room, fanning fears and uncertainty. Yet despite all of the flux and change, it is created by people, and people will continue to find a place for themselves in this new, evolving workplace. The bright spot in the future of work is that our jobs will rely on becoming more human, self-aware, connected, and collaborative. That shift, whether big or small, will be much less traumatic with a firm footing in a full life.

When I began interviewing people for this book, I expected to find people in the second half of their careers wanting to slow down and relax. To my surprise, they were ambitious and wanted to do more. They wanted to keep learning and adapting and squeeze every drop of juice out of life.

This book is not a step-by-step guide that will get you to that promised land, but it will help you get unstuck and help you figure out how to find your own path to work with more joy, meaning, and purpose. Since that TEDx talk in 2016, I've expanded my own knowledge of investing in life and have leveraged my three decades of experience as a workplace innovator and entrepreneur, shifting my career toward helping other people navigate their futures at work in a way that's fulfilling and sustainable.

WHAT'S IN THIS BOOK—AND NOT IN THIS BOOK

This is not a book of theory. I'm not an academic, and I haven't done loads of statistically balanced research on workplace trends. I have read hundreds of books and research reports, interviewed people across the world who seem to have gotten it right, and experienced enough to provide the broad brushstrokes of what's happening now and what's coming for people struggling with a professional life that's left them unfulfilled. I've combined many of the stories I've seen, heard, and lived firsthand with the latest data and research to show you that a better path is possible. After reading this, you will have a better understanding of the mindset shift required, along with some tangible, actionable techniques, to help you forge your own path, invest in your life, and future-proof your career with meaning, joy, and purpose. You should have a clear idea of the steps you can take to live life on your own terms.

PART I

LEARN: HOW AND WHY THE WORLD OF WORK IS CHANGING

Four forces are colliding and transforming the global economy: the rise of emerging markets, the accelerating impact of technology on the natural forces of market competition, an aging world population, and accelerating flows of trade, capital, people and data.

—RICHARD DOBBS, JAMES MANYIKA, AND JONATHAN WOETZEL, *NO ORDINARY DISRUPTION: THE FOUR GLOBAL FORCES BREAKING ALL THE TRENDS*

We've seen the headlines about the future of work and are well prepared. Or are we? We've gone from automating factories to virtual surgeons. In Part I, *Learn*, we'll learn how the world of work is changing in ways that are profoundly impacting professionals at all levels.

CHAPTER 1

THE FUTURE OF WORK

The automation of factories has already decimated jobs in traditional manufacturing, and the rise of artificial intelligence is likely to extend this job destruction...with only the most caring, creative, or supervisory roles remaining.[1]

—STEPHEN HAWKING

Robot automation will take 800 million jobs by 2030.[2]

—MCKINSEY GLOBAL INSTITUTE

Globalization, disruption, and longevity are coming together to transform the way we work and the way people see the future of work. Mostly, we see the future

---

1 Stephen Hawking, "This is the most dangerous time for our planet," *The Guardian*, December 1, 2016, accessed September 21, 2018, https://www.theguardian.com/commentisfree/2016/dec/01/stephen-hawking-dangerous-time-planet-inequality.

2 British Broadcasting Corporation, "Robot automation will 'take 800 million jobs by 2030' – report," *BBC.com*, November 29, 2017, accessed September 14, 2018, https://www.bbc.com/news/world-us-canada-42170100.

of work as bewildering. The perpetual mention of accelerating change gives us motion sickness. Our eyes glaze over reading the doomsday headlines in the press about the company that transferred all its factory jobs to the Philippines and closed the local plant; the two-hundred-year-old institution that went out of business in what seems like an instant.

The arguments for and against artificial intelligence, robotics, and trade are so complex and abstract it is hard to relate them to our own lives.

What does it really have to do with us?

We have travelled the world. We've managed remote teams in India or the Philippines. Change doesn't make us quake. We've taken that executive MBA course on technology disruption at business school. The new digital strategy was a big win this year. We even have a personal assistant/PR department/intern/niece who set up our Instagram account.

Yet, we wonder in darker moments where it's all leading. If we all live to one hundred, will we still be sitting at the same desk, slowly withering away as work becomes more tedious and insane? Can we afford to do anything else?

Beyond the headlines, there are the real-life impacts

that we experience—the 6 a.m. conference calls (is it so much to ask to have breakfast with our kids or spouse a few times a week?). The to-do list that exceeds the day's capacity from the first email as we try to operate at full speed on three time zones with competing agendas. Now, there is even Wi-Fi on the plane, so that long flight we used to use for catch-up (or movie binges) is still about work and quelling the latest fire.

The robots may not be banging down the door for most executives. But we're also not exactly living four-hour workweeks, typing away on our laptop from a café in Paris, or taking time off for the things we said we would do—write a book, road trip down the coast, run a marathon—taking advantage of a longer life and longer career. We are "busy" and "fine" and not looking too far down the road.

Time to wake up. As it says in one of many forecasts about what skills we'll need in the future, "Highly mobile, digitally savvy, agile adapters will be the new elite."[3] If we're ambitious, we want to stay ahead of the curve. For now, the best way to equip ourselves for dealing with all the changes is by seeking to understand them and the effects they may have on us.

---

3 4IR.org Newsdesk, "Futures of Work: Lifelong Learning is the New Black," *4IR.org*, 2018, accessed September 21, 2018, https://www.the4thindustrialrevolution.org/the-world-economic-forums-8-futures-of-work-lifelong-learning-is-the-new-black.

The world is changing faster, and most of us have been too busy to realize the cost of the acceleration and the fact that our longer lives require a new approach: a future-proof approach.

First, let's define what we mean by these key driving forces affecting the future world of work.

WORKING IN A DISRUPTIVE WORLD

Between globalization, disruption, and longevity, disruption is the element of change most prevalent in the business media. There's a lot of talk about automation and its effect on the workplace, startups with lean teams challenging and conquering incumbents, and whole industries being displaced by shifts in consumer demand. Across the world, the lifespan of a corporation has declined. Innovation consulting firm Innosight notes that the average tenure of a firm in the S&P 500 was twenty-four years in 2016 and is forecast to halve by 2027.[4]

In some ways, disruption isn't new and it's largely productive. I remember at the age of twenty-one, I astonished the staff in Henry Kissinger's office when I showed them how to get off the typewriter and do a mail merge on MS-DOS.

4 Scott D. Anthony, S. Patrick Viguerie, Evan I. Schwartz and John Van Landeghem, "2018 Corporate Longevity Forecast: Creative Destruction is Accelerating," *Innosite.com*, accessed September 21, 2018, https://www.innosight.com/insight/creative-destruction.

In the media industry, I saw firsthand the successful adoption of technology at Time Warner's electronic publishing unit. We were one of the first to have audiobooks, then CD-ROMs, and CD-ROMs connected to websites. We made electronic games and did author chats online, sometimes with staff sending in the questions to make sure it all looked "live," but it was cutting-edge at the time. We even had a guy building a CD-ROM of the human body. Rumor had it, he had somehow gotten ahold of a cadaver and sliced it into millimeter strips to scan into a computer. Now we can be on a beach in Thailand and borrow a digital medical book from a library in Seattle, with no human casualties in the process.

Now there is disruptive innovation everywhere. In the medical field, diagnoses are being done by computers in a much faster, and sometimes better, way than doctors. Doctors certainly won't go away, but their roles are changing. My father is a highly educated and skilled psychiatrist, and talk therapy is one profession we thought would never be replaced by a robot. Yet, a study revealed that many people feel more comfortable talking about their problems to a robot than a human doctor, and mental health chatbots are proving effective at meeting people where they are (their phones!).[5] Human empathy has its

5 The Economist, "The computer will see you now," *Economist.com*, August 20, 2014, accessed September 21, 2018, https://www.economist.com/science-and-technology/2014/08/20/the-computer-will-see-you-now.

unique place, of course, but the reality is that people feel less judged by a robot and are more likely to open up in an honest way. Humans and machines together can drive better outcomes and are changing where we add value.

Even the once-staid legal profession has been subject to dramatic changes. Lawyers today have instant access to a wealth of information available electronically, which has contributed to a reduction of law firm associates now replaced by automation. The industry is at a crossroads in how to utilize people and determining how best to utilize people and fill their clients' needs. Eversheds Sutherland law firm started ES Agile, which provides lawyers to in-house legal teams. The lawyers work on a temporary contract basis, allowing them more flexibility in their schedules. As Eversheds partner, Jennifer Van Dale, has said, "Technology is not the future of work, it is the present of work."[6]

In every industry, companies are under pressure to be agile and competitive, and they don't always have a technological edge, so the pressure shifts to the employees. People must sometimes work strange hours, and there's a prevalent, underlying concern for job security. In a cup half-empty outlook, this all appears to be negatively disrupting the natural order of things. However, much of the

6 Jennifer Van Dale (the future of work), interviewed by Diana Wu David of Future Proof, March 28, 2018.

change enhances the human-added value of jobs, and this is what we must realize, accept, and adapt to.

GLOBALIZATION: IT'S A SMALL WORLD AFTER ALL

The trend for companies is expansion into new markets for growth, cost reduction, and flexibility. Chinese companies are going global.[7] Western companies, seeing revenues shift to emerging markets, are scrambling to find board directors from those regions. Businesses used to outsource processes to low income countries, but today those countries are moving up the value chain. Flexibility is enhanced by technology to access the best talent anywhere in the world, and some companies have sourced their entire staff from freelancers. The trend is for companies to be global, even at the small and startup size.

Globalization affects corporate policy and practice with a profound impact on our day-to-day work from dual-career couples chasing work opportunities across continents to those infamous late-night conference calls. Will we be signed on as an expat and get six-weeks' paid holiday and nine-months' maternity leave or signed on as a local with less generous policies? I remember the shock my colleagues from the editorial department had at

7 Scott Cendrowski, "How 5 Chinese Companies Became Global Giants," *Fortune.com*, June 24, 2016, accessed September 21, 2018, http://fortune.com/2016/06/24/chinese-global-xiaomi.

Financial Times when they found out I had an eight-week statutory maternity leave instead of the nine months our colleagues received in the UK. Now, just a decade later, *Financial Times* has standardized global maternity leave at twenty weeks, making them a leader in the global trend toward better policies for families across a global workforce.[8]

This is a world that most leaders couldn't even imagine in the recent past. Some people would rather not deal with all of the complexity and just want to open a bookstore or a cupcake shop on the corner. Yet, the harsh reality is that even at the local level, commodity prices can have a huge effect on the purchase of wheat, fuel, paper, and any number of other business needs. It's important not to take it for granted and realize we have a great advantage if we can navigate these waters.

Speaking of bakeries, I spoke to a board member of a 300-strong South African bakery chain, which learned dramatically how interconnectedness impacts business regulation on a larger scale. All the bread in one of their neighborhood bakeries was priced the same as nearby shops, and what began as a bunch of local managers chatting about the price of bread turned into a price-fixing scandal. The entire chain—all 300 stores—was handed

8 Financial Times, "About Us," *FT.com*, accessed September 21, 2018, https://aboutus.ft.com/en-gb/careers/culture-and-benefits.

a 10 percent fine on their profits. That's a hard lesson learned and an ideal example illustrating that we're not just a carefree owner of a neighborhood business; everything is interconnected, and we need to be aware of that to run our work and personal lives in ways that take advantage of globalization, rather than become a victim of it.

LONGEVITY AND THE 100-YEAR LIFE

Governments, companies, and individuals are grappling with lifespans that are edging up to triple digits as we prolong life, and quality of life, ever longer. If a child born in the West today has a fifty-fifty chance of living beyond 105, and many of us can work well into our seventies and eighties, we may need to reassess what we are all in such a rush about.

Part of the frenzy may be well-justified fear. Longer lives mean a need for more capital accumulation and preservation as our world shifts away from the security of unstable pensions. The World Economic Forum has spoken of a "global retirement timebomb," with developed countries needing to hike their retirement ages before their pension systems collapse. Just eight countries—the US, UK, Japan, Canada, Australia, India, China, and the Netherlands—face a combined shortfall of $400 trillion by 2050. In "advanced economies," the official retirement ages of sixty-five for men and sixty-three for women are being reviewed, with the Forum recommending that most people work until at least seventy.[9]

Senior citizens are taking note and keeping busy, for financial reasons and because they are healthier and more active, so they can work longer and enjoy contributing. In the year 2000, just under 13 percent of Americans sixty-five and over reported being employed full- or part-time. By May 2016, that figure had jumped to 18.8 percent—meaning that nearly nine million Americans sixty-five-plus were gainfully employed. Over the next five years, that number is expected to increase to 32 percent.[10] Across the world, initiatives such as "Retired Not Out" platforms and free university classes for senior citizens are being piloted to help us work longer, better.

On a very personal level, however, longevity, rising healthcare costs, and declining pensions are resulting in a rethink about how we manage our careers. The days of learn, work, retire are gone. Lifelong learning is the new mantra. Fortunately, working longer has its advantages, because those additional years mean we don't always

---

9 Ivana Kottasová, "Global retirement 'timebomb': Why you'll have to work past 70," *CNN Money*, May 26, 2017, accessed September 21, 2018, http://money.cnn.com/2017/05/26/pf/retirement-age-70-pensions/index.html.

10 John Hanc, "Workers Are Working Longer — and Better," *The New York Times*, March 2, 2017, accessed September 21, 2018, https://www.nytimes.com/2017/03/02/business/retirement/workers-are-working-longer-and-better.html.

have to do everything right now. Work may start to resemble something more like tours of duty with meaningful breaks in between for learning, caring, or renewing.

SUCCESS: A PYRRHIC VICTORY?

At this point, you might be saying to yourself, "It's a scary world out there and I'm lucky to be gainfully employed and at the top of my game. Why mess with that!?" True! I am not interested in telling you to dump your whole career and become a basket weaver on the beach in Thailand (unless that is truly what you want to do). I am telling you that you can't just stick your head in the sand and hope past success carries you through another thirty years without a process and a plan. That's why I wrote this book. Like it or not, globalization, technology, and longevity will have a profound effect on our careers and personal lives. Ignore them at your peril.

Globalization means we're always on. Technology means we're always on. The disruption of those industries means we're always slightly paranoid. Former Intel CEO Andrew Grove set the stage for this era in his highly acclaimed book, *Only the Paranoid Survive.*[11] Two decades on, it is more true than ever.

---

11 Andrew S. Grove, *Only the Paranoid Survive: How to Exploit the Crisis Points That Challenge Every Company* (New York: Random House, 1999).

Technology has changed expectations in the workplace because employers always have access to their employees, and employees have fewer viable excuses for not being available for work. Globalization breaks the boundaries of time in good ways and bad. It's great to be able to have a productive conference call any time of the day, but we need to reconsider the value we bring to those calls. Now, being a team player isn't simply a next-door neighbor kind of trait, it means developing global, virtual traits that will help us succeed in this environment.

What is the cost of this culture of optimization? Despite technology's conveniences to bring everyone together, there are many human-based problems created by adapting to this new reality. If we need to be paranoid to survive, then anxiety is our perpetual consort. As a society, that is reflected in a raft of issues from mental health problems to just plain disengagement. Harvard Business School professor Clayton Christensen in his book *How Will You Measure Your Life?* talks about seeing his incredibly high-profile Harvard classmates succeed in business only to fall prey to failed relationships, wandering integrity, and a deep sense of emptiness.[12]

The often-cited survey about employee engagement from the esteemed Gallup research organization bears this out, citing only 13 percent of people are engaged in

12 Clayton M. Christensen, *How Will You Measure Your Life?* (New York: Harper Collins, 2012).

their work.[13] More shocking is a recent book from Stanford professor Jeffrey Pfeffer called *Dying for a Paycheck* that claims work is killing us.[14] People aren't engaged in their companies, and the increase in freelancing is leading to increased economic insecurity, less wage growth, and stress.

WHEN "HAVING IT ALL" RINGS HOLLOW

My first boss at *Financial Times*, Su-Mei Thompson, was a notoriously hard worker, and though incredibly supportive and instrumental in my and others' ability to weather family commitments, she set the bar high. Even pregnancy didn't slow her down. She was rumored to be on her BlackBerry an hour after her C-section. I had eight weeks' recovery scheduled after my pregnancy but went back early when senior management came to town. That was the prevailing trend in those days—and is still a reality for many executives. A company's policy may allow a new parent a reasonable amount of time off, but the reality is we are expected to be working whenever the company needs us. Either the structure of work doesn't allow, or we are too ambitious to miss a visit from top management or a big client. The flexibility now is better,

13 Gallup, "The Engaged Workplace," *Gallup.com*, accessed September 21, 2018.

14 Jeffrey Pfeffer, "Dying for a Paycheck,", *Stanford Graduate School of Business*, March 20, 2018, accessed September 21, 2018, https://www.gsb.stanford.edu/faculty-research/books/dying-paycheck.

but we often don't let ourselves take the time because of fear of missing out on promotions or in anticipation of judgment that will affect our career or business for the worse.

Many factors contribute to a negative impact in today's always-connected work environment. Late night or early morning conference calls at least once a week are a norm for most of the people I know. I remember sitting in the nursery, in the dark, settling my child in for sleep, talking in an overworked mom's lullaby: "You're okay, honey. Mommy is putting you to bed. Don't mind me scrolling through the agenda and notes for tonight's meeting."

My "Pyrrhic victory," the glance back at the battlefield to see the carcasses piled high, was punctuated by my best friend's suicide. Yet, so many small things—which in hindsight weren't small at all—had been adding up to a life that didn't fit the one I wanted to build:

- The walking pneumonia I got trying to take the kids to see my parents in America, moving to a new apartment, and closing a big project at work all in one month.
- The night in a hospital in Shanghai, convinced I had kidney failure, which turned out to be back spasms from too much travel.
- Flying at almost eight months pregnant on a red-eye

flight to Sydney, Australia to fire someone over lunch and getting back on the next flight, exhausted and hoping I didn't give birth on the plane.

- The time my young daughter complained of a toothache, and I suddenly realized we hadn't been to the dentist for two years because we moved and the postcard reminders were going to the old house. Her baby molars were so rotten that she had to be put under general anesthetic to crack them out of her jaw. The day of the operation I held her hand as the dentist and three nurses crowded around looking at me with what I was sure was awe at my complete lack of parenting skill. Who would let their kid's teeth rot like that!? In those moments I would think to myself, "What am I doing?"

I am not the only one. Sophia Yap, producer of the Path of Victors reality show, said that she recently celebrated her first ever Mother's Day with her teenage daughter. Previously, she had always been travelling for her work as a corporate lawyer. Commuting to a different city or country to work is becoming more common; the very worst example I know of is a banker whose family lived in Connecticut while he commuted to his position in Hong Kong. Just a few weeks ago, a good friend cancelled our dinner. She had been travelling like mad and, on her flight back from the US, she passed out, slammed into the steward's trolley, and spent two weeks in the hospital recovering from fifteen fractures to her face, jawbone, and skull. Enough missed birthdays and near-misses and the idea of "having it all" rings hollow.

SHIFTING MINDSETS TO MOVE FORWARD

So where do we go from here? The good news is that the future of work is not a clarion call for our demise. It's our magic portal to more balance and rhythm in our lives. We can adapt our job-based mindset and evolve the skills needed to keep pace and keep peace.

One shift is from a linear path to one of agility and experimentation. Adopting the agile mindset used in business innovation, we can experiment in our work projects and in finding new opportunities to apply our knowledge and passion. Instead of work, earn, retire, we have time for exploration. For example, in the past we might learn the lifetime value of a customer in marketing class and apply that knowledge with small iterations for thirty years. Today, it's all about perpetual testing, getting data back, and trying it again. We learn how to learn, repackage, and add value and relevance to serve the company's, customer's, and society's changing needs. In doing so, we can more flexibly serve our own needs. This is a mindset shift we will talk about in more detail in chapters to come.

Another shift is from hierarchy to networks. Harvard

Professor John P. Kotter noticed this shift and described how hierarchies coexist with networks in his book *Accelerate: Building Strategic Agility for a Faster-Moving World*.[15] Enabling technologies such as 5G on the horizon, interaction through Slack, Trello, or Google documents, and new platforms like Upwork and Fiverr or memberships like Onda Life are making the idea of working from the beach or co-working spaces around the world seem more commonplace and effective. Our tribes of trusted collaborators become more interesting than who is on what level of the company organizational chart.

Technology enables crowdsourcing of ideas as well. From hackathons to Kickstarter, crowdsourcing offers everything from basic funding to collaborative tools to bring products, services, and solutions to life. For example, one of my fellow TEDx speakers invented a type of citizen science that allows people to use a snorkeling mask to measure ocean temperatures, aggregate that data to the cloud, and help understand temperature changes in oceans around the world. On a more basic level, *Financial Times* has a philanthropy program where staff around the world vote for the company's seasonal appeal, which directs millions of dollars in annual charitable giving. As we try to harness this power, our social capital, or the ability to connect to people in different ways, becomes more

---

15 John P. Kotter, *Accelerate: Building Strategic Agility for a Faster-Moving World* (Boston: Harvard Business School, 2014).

important to achieve as well as learn. General Motors Corporation Chief Talent Officer, Michael Arena, dubs social capital "the competitive advantage that is created based on the way an individual is connected to others" and a requirement for innovation.[16] You'll hear another example of the power of connections from Brian Tang, who has mastered collaboration across his networks, further on in this chapter.

Finally, there is a shift to agency over one's own career and brand. In order to leverage all of the experience and intelligence across multiple jobs, geographies, and careers, we need to get a good sense of what our strengths are, where we contribute, and who we need to partner with to shore up our blind spots or unknowns. If we can understand the value we bring to people and projects, and communicate that broadly, we can be prepared to fight for the balance we need.

SOFT SKILLS ARE THE NEW CAREER MAKERS

Forget reading, writing, and arithmetic as the single golden ticket to success. According to the World Economic Forum, OECD, and the Institute of the Future, mindset shift should also embrace so-called "soft skills,"

---

16 Michael Arena, "Social Capital: The Next Frontier for HR," *HR Exchange Network*, October 2, 2018, accessed October 28, 2018, https://www.hrexchangenetwork.com/people-analytics/articles/social-capital-the-next-frontier-for-hr.

personal attributes that enable someone to interact effectively and harmoniously with other people, as the new career makers in the twenty-first century. Character traits and competencies including creativity, collaboration, adaptability, and initiative make up the increasingly popular future skills, indices driving new educational assessments and hiring practices.[17]

This is a departure from past requirements in the workplace. If we have one job at one company in one town, we learn how to relate to people in one way. If we must relate to many different people in different countries or switch careers from high tech to education, or finance to hospitality, we need to adjust our language and frameworks. People have more careers in their lifetimes than in the past, and that requires fundamentally changing skillsets, especially in working with people. As we can see around us, social organization is changing and will change more in the future. Where once it was rude to send an email instead of a letter, multi-million-dollar businesses in China are now run on the instant messaging platform WeChat. Not only must we master the technology, but also the new social mores and opportunities that accompany it.

---

17 Organisation for Economic Co-operation and Development (OECD), "Future of Work and Skills," *oecd.org*, 2017, accessed September 21, 2018, https://www.oecd.org/els/emp/wcms_556984.pdf.

It seems straightforward. We put a man on the moon; surely, we can train people to communicate clearly with other people. Yet we have a hard enough time with our own family, much less with people from other walks of life. Soft skills are incredibly important as we move from one job or office to another with dramatically different cultures. More companies are globalizing as well. It used to be the norm for big companies like Microsoft to have multiple offices around the world, but technology and globalization allows big *and* small companies to use the same infrastructure models.

We could be a corporate coach in Los Angeles with clients in the US and Europe, a virtual assistant in the Philippines, and have our website design done in Ukraine. Beyond the corporate world, globalization requires us to work together in new ways to tackle the big problems. We need new combinations of people speaking to and collaborating with each other around the world.

¿HABLAS FUTURE OF WORK?

Communication is another critical element of thriving with globalization. Some people are very direct and expressive in their communication; others might be indirect and expressive or indirect and non-expressive.[18]

---

18 Mitchell R. Hammer, "Intercultural Conflict Style Inventory," *ICS Inventory*, January 2016, accessed November 17, 2018 https://icsinventory.com.

In the United States, particularly in the business world, being very direct is a virtue; but it is often not a virtue outside of the country. A colleague might feel they've told us what we need to know but thought it would be rude to be direct. In turn, we feel they're hiding things from us, while they feel that we just don't get it. Without awareness, this is another way globalization can cause problems.

I worked with an American and a Brit on a team, and they always had trouble with their respective ways of doing things. The Brit didn't care for the American's habit of sending emails without starting with, "Dear Bob, how are you?" and signing off with, "Best regards, Jane."

The Brit said, "Wow, I just find him so abrupt and rude," while the American replied, "We don't have time for all that. What's the point?"

Even between two cultures that we might think are quite similar, it's important to be aware of these types of differences and to be compassionate. For example, a gentleman is chairman of one company in Australia and another company in Malaysia. When he chairs meetings in Malaysia and has an idea to discuss, he asks his staff for their opinions, beginning with those with the lowest seniority and working up to those with the highest seniority. At the end, he shares his own thoughts. If he wanted to discuss the same idea at the Australian company, he would present his idea first and then let everyone jump in and critique the idea and give their views.

In both meetings, this is the same person working in the same role, but he's learned to adapt to different cultures. He knows that in Malaysia people have a respect for power, distance, authority, and hierarchy. If he put his idea out there first, nobody would ever disagree with him. If we're at the helm and it's our first time in Malaysia and everyone immediately agrees with us, we might think we just had the best idea around, when in fact, we're just operating in a different cultural context.

It's not our way or the highway; there are certain international standards, but everyone has their own speed limits, traffic patterns, and shortcuts.

VODKA IN SPACE

Trust plays a big part in rewarding relationships, and cultures view trust in different ways. Americans often view transparency as a measure of trust, whereas other cultures might view safety as a gauge of trust: "If you promise me I'll be safe, then I will trust you."

Other times, there is trust in clear hierarchy or teamwork. A great example of communication and trust is when the Russian and American astronauts went into space together. Before the trip, the teams met, and the Russians said in so many words, “Hey, it’s great to see you. Let’s drink some vodka. It’s all going to be great.”

The Americans were all business: “Have you checked all the switches? We just want to be sure everything’s okay.” The Russians were very expressive, and the Americans thought they were crazy. “We can’t go into space with these guys; they’re going to be drunk all the time.”

The Russians looked at the Americans in a similar light. “They have no passion for this mission. We can’t go into space with these guys. They’re like robots; what if something happens that’s not on the checklist? We can’t rely on them.”

This is an offbeat look at trust in relationships, but it shows how important it is to understand your team, its goals, and your audience.

EMBRACE VIRTUALITY

The combination of global and tech creates a virtual disconnect. Virtual teams are scattered across towns, across the country, or around the world. A lot of information can go undetected on calls when we don’t have time for idle but beneficial conversation, or when the connection is poor. In other cases, it is difficult to get to know other staff and share highlights of, say, your trip to Hawaii because you're talking to someone on a different planet relative to their lifestyle and responsibilities.

It's very important to fully understand what brings people together on a team. Have face-to-face interactions, even via video calls, as often as possible; understand each person's motivation and desires; learn what each of us is bringing to the team; assess work expectations and ethics. This is time well spent, especially with the traditional high turnover within virtual teams spread across multiple countries.

It's a valuable skill for us as professionals, and as people, to take the time and set the expectation that we will be understanding of each person's individual roles and desires, and the work required to bring it together. These connections may stand us in good stead for future projects. The experience may also be useful when we are the one looking for flexibility in our work and can understand what it means to be a good virtual team member.

LEARNING FROM CORPORATE INNOVATION

Clayton Christensen is the godfather, if you will, of disruption. His book, *The Innovator's Dilemma*, talks about how established corporations are set up for efficiency in the way they are organized around producing output at scale. Yet they fail to recognize disruptive competitors. The disruption may start in a small, niche market they don't really care about, and with a product that's not that great. A newer company enters the market with the ability to iterate at lower cost and can quickly overtake the legacy player. The solution behind this has been to innovate at the fringes. Fifteen or twenty years ago, businesses commonly set up small labs where they could disrupt themselves.

This still occurs today to some extent, and I think it parallels our individual careers. If we have career capital built up, we generally have high expectations in terms of prestige, income, and cost structure, but we have to think about what a disruption will mean to our career and overall life, and proactively disrupt ourselves to stay competitive and employable.

In the same way as companies do, individuals can continue to leverage career capital and networks and iterate at the margins. We can think about ways to adapt by experimenting with and applying current assets or skills, or by learning new ones. It's easy to be overwhelmed by globalization and technology, but if we understand the value we add to our job, we can leverage that value to make work more human.

For example, I've crafted my career and my life to leverage my network of connections, which are important to raise awareness for board training and to build a community of people working for better corporate governance. I know my ability to relate to senior level people and my teaching skills are valuable. Character, calmness, and strategic thinking also have an influence. Because of today's technology, I can travel and do many different things while still providing that value to my job, employers, and clients from anywhere in the world. This facet of today's business world is affecting every industry, from large, multi-national corporations to tiny, work-from-home businesses.

Hopefully, we've peaked in this frenzy of fear, disruption, and technology, realizing that, though some jobs will change and others will go away, we have an opportunity to take advantage of this new environment. A willingness to adapt to changes and fail fast at the margins can allow us to move forward with new courage.

BECOMING YOU, INC.

There is a tendency to focus on a job title and be content with the label someone has created for us to explain "this is what I do," but we bring much more to a position than the title. As leaders, we have more skills than running meetings and training staff on day-to-day tasks. You are more than your job, so don't be fearful of losing it to automation. Machine language doesn't have your leadership skills to run a team in China. Examine your entire quiver of skills and capitalize on them.

Feeling under pressure or second fiddle to technology particularly impacts senior corporate executives because they've learned to see themselves in the context of their functional work. "I'm a good financial trader." Okay, you're good at trading, but what makes you that way? You have reflexes to make quick decisions and you're calm under pressure; those are valuable attributes.

I see this in senior leaders looking toward their next career chapter. They have reached the pinnacle of their work in one company or industry, and they've decided they want new challenges, maybe even in a new industry. Let's say Margaret was head of investment banking at MoneyTree Financial and now she's considering a board role at a defense industry company. Understanding her own character traits is a huge asset as she begins to navigate her future work.

In my case, I'd like to do more cutting-edge technology work. Seeking out opportunities, such as a board role in robotics education, allows me the opportunity to learn new subject areas and contribute existing skills.

Understanding your core skills and expertise and how

they apply to other situations is an important first step. Reputations are incredibly important in this age of social media. It's critical to cultivate our personal brand—what we stand for—and to be more aware of ourselves and how other people perceive us. Attitude and professionalism are crucial in times of change. The ability to hit the ground running and develop collaboration skills goes a long way. The networks within our companies and outside of it are very important for our careers, particularly for solving problems at our companies and in our industries or communities.

Amy Bevilacqua is a friend of mine with a glorious career at the Public Broadcasting System and in film. She also has a passion for education. Amy applied that interest and her skills to a new role as chief innovation officer for a university, leading both strategy and investments. When I asked her how she got this plum position, she said, "I worked for a company that I thought was fantastic, but then the whole thing blew up. We had to do a lot of cleanup and I just dug in and did the right thing. I never expected anything good to come of it. Maybe I had some lessons learned, but that was a pivotal point in my life, cementing my reputation as somebody who was smart and committed and could get the job done under adverse circumstances. People on the board of this company noticed that drive, and that's how I got my new job."[19]

19 Amy Bevilacqua (innovation), interviewed by Diana Wu David of Future Proof, October 31, 2018.

Amy's a perfect example of how being agile, adaptable, and rolling with the punches can lead to success.

At the end of the day, ownership of our career is not something we can wait to be given to us. The responsibility to create our career, what sacrifices we make for it, and how it fits into our life rests with us.

LONGEVITY INSPIRES NEW OPPORTUNITY

Mid- to late-career people and those approaching retirement are becoming aware that longevity is the issue of our time. People are simply living longer and the economics of learning at school, working forty years, and retiring for twenty don't work.

The good news is much insight into longevity has been brought to public attention by Lynda Gratton and Andrew Scott, authors of *The 100-Year Life: Living and Working in an Age of Longevity*. In their book, they talk optimistically about real changes in people's lives: "You now have the potential for a more stimulating future as a result of having more time."[20] I'd like to add that we have a more stimulating *present* as a result of knowing we have more time. We can take more time to enjoy life as a journey: live each day, pursue multiple talents and roles, take a sabbatical. If we know we're going to be working long

20 Lynda Gratton and Andrew Scott, *The 100-Year Life* (London: Bloomsbury, 2016).

past age sixty, maybe we don't need to climb the corporate ladder in such a hurry, postponing our bucket list to retirement.

Consider maternity leave. There was a time, partly because there weren't as many women working, when we were not allowed time off for maternity (or paternity) leave. Today, people think more along the lines of, "I'm going to live a long life and I'll be working for most of it, so I'll take time when I need it." That's important, because we'll need to take time to stay current and learn, and the cycle will be more of learn, do, reflect.

Taking time off for the birth of a child, family sickness, and other significant life issues is already more prevalent than in the past and this trend will continue. Of course, we can't ignore the financial aspect of this equation. People still need to work, and we will need to plan on working longer, structuring life with the understanding that in later years we won't have the stamina but will want to intellectually continue working and contributing. It will be financially advantageous to have an income stream, and more rewarding to continue being productive than spending decades playing bingo or binge-watching Netflix.

If sixty years is the new normal span for a working life, we'll have more opportunity to experiment, make some mistakes and recover. We might have multiple careers, with sabbaticals or time off for further education in between. That leaves time to explore other passions and interests and take time to be with our friends and family. These trends give us opportunity to pause and focus some energy in other important areas of our lives.

THE HALFTIME LOCKER ROOM TALK

In his book *Halftime: Changing Your Game Plan from Success to Significance*, Bob Buford talks about the second half of life and taking the time to reflect on values. He says, "...for the second half of life to be better than the first, you must make the choice to step outside of the safety of living on autopilot. You must wrestle with who you are, why you believe what you've professed to believe about your life, and what you do to provide meaning and structure to your daily activities and relationships."[21]

He was mainly talking about retirement, but I believe that today what we're really talking about is taking a break in the game to make sure we're engaged. We should be stepping outside our comfort zones and providing meaning and structure on an ongoing basis. What I've found is many people are looking at their second half in their 40s—not preparing to retire but planning other ambitious

21 Bob Buford, *Halftime: Changing Your Game Plan from Success to Significance* (Grand Rapids: Zondervan, 1997), 36.

endeavors during what some people have begun to call the midlife marathon years. Let's look at a pair of high-achieving examples.

BRIAN TANG GETS A SECOND WIND

Brian Tang had worked at white-shoe law firm Sullivan & Cromwell on Wall Street and in Silicon Valley during the dotcom boom and then at global investment bank Credit Suisse in Hong Kong where he helped establish its Chinese investment banking joint venture and participated in some of the largest IPOs in the world. Professionally, it likely wouldn't get any better than that. He had young kids at home and found himself thinking about how he could best be an example to them and continue to grow and make an impact.

He knew he was already working at the top of his game in his given market but could see that the marketplace was rapidly changing. He still had quite a few years in his career ahead of him and he asked, "How can I best contribute to make the most impact?" One thing he observed was how the financial crisis was largely attributable to conduct risk that arose within the highly competitive financial industry, and that more rules and fines by regulators were not the main solution. There was a limit as to what he could do from within his company, and so he set up and launched Asia Capital Markets Institute (ACMI) at the Hong Kong Stock Exchange, or as he describes it, "left an aircraft carrier to try to herd the fleet." He felt that he could use his knowledge, experience, and networks in ways that could shepherd his industry and, in turn, the financing of the real economy, to a better place. With the advent in recent years of fintech, AI, and blockchain, Tang's initiative has since pivoted to also focus on other areas, such as online capital marketplaces (crowdfunding and token sales), RegTech, and AI governance.

Tang's interest in social innovation and impact were a second motivation. At Credit Suisse, Tang was also the co-chairman of the Hong Kong Charity Committee and president of the Asia-Pacific Microfinance Advocates, and so saw the benefits, and limitations, of philanthropy. He initially wanted to set up a legal clearinghouse to support social entrepreneurs in Asia, but when he learned that another organization was planning the same, he instead started Young Makers & ChangeMakers, an inclusive education platform and community to foster young maker mindsets, STEAM education, and twenty-first century skills. Originally inspired by his own kids, the social enterprise now includes their innovative Technovation x #GirlsMakeTech program, which has engaged more than fifty schools to create mobile apps to address the UN Sustainable Development Goals and resulted in a team of Hong Kong secondary students winning the global top junior prize at the World Pitch Summit held at Google's Mountainview headquarters.

Tang's youth development initiatives have also included organizing Hong Kong's first LegalTech and RegTech Hackathon, where Hong Kong law students ultimately won at the Global Legal Hackathon in New York with their AI tool to improve access to justice, as well as facilitating middle school student experiments that were selected and launched into space on a NASA sounding rocket from NASA Wallops Flight Facility during the summer of 2018. Most recently, Tang has been appointed by Hong Kong University to spearhead a new interdisciplinary Law, Innovation, Technology, and Entrepreneurship (LITE) program to help university students better prepare for the jobs of tomorrow. Working with the private sector, government, and now, academia, Tang is constantly learning and working with different stakeholders to solve difficult problems in new ways. As this process evolves, he finds combining his existing skills and networks with a willingness to adapt to be unique, fulfilling, and in demand.[22]

MARK PIESANEN EMBRACES DISRUPTION

Mark is an example of someone who has adapted to today's markets. He's adept at transitioning to the next place where he can maximize his potential. I met Mark when he was a journalist and the recipient of the Knight Bagehot Fellowship, which had earned him

22 Brian Tang (social innovation and impact), interviewed by Diana Wu David of Future Proof, March 5, 2018.

a full, one-year scholarship in business school. He'd already notched some enviable wins as a reporter for his coverage of the Enron collapse, and during tours as a foreign correspondent.

Mark realized he was at the apex of his journalism career. With a host of skills and a knack for working with people, he wanted to apply his talent in a new way, exploring different opportunities. After school, he turned to management consulting and then landed a business development role at Google. When he came to this point, the work seemed insurmountable. He was a journalist surrounded by business people, yet he climbed to new heights, working for a company everyone wants to work for, and achieved a measure of financial stability that would have been difficult to meet as a journalist. The position refreshed his career and he had a lot of fun, but eventually, Mark felt he had reached a roadblock.

He left Google and joined a startup, moving to a COO role with TouchCast, a company whose technology transforms businesses' communication and collaboration via smart video. With this new role, Mark has had all kinds of new adventures working in China and other places around the world, defining a new industry.[23]

---

23 Mark Piesanen (disruption), interviewed by Diana Wu David of Future Proof, September 21, 2018.

He embraced disruption rather than bemoan it and became what cultural critic and author Po Bronson calls a "boom rider." Be it digital media or the evolution of radio to television and television to the internet, the reality is that "boom" implies "bust." To catch the wave, we have to follow current and breaking trends, and discover what we can do better.

USING VOLATILITY TO OUR ADVANTAGE

In light of new industries and the way work is shifting, it's up to each individual to connect the dots and not be too literal in tailoring their skill sets. If you're a writer, that doesn't mean you can *only* be a writer. Broadly consider all of the traits that apply to your career in the context of where the world is heading. Embrace lateral thinking and leverage your networks in each new career chapter.

Resilience and responsibility are fundamental values that can anchor a fulfilling life. Be entrepreneurial with your career and take stock of what you're bringing to the table. In many instances, people consider their company as a father figure that will take care of them. While sometimes that is the case, we must always look out for ourselves.

I worked with a company that presented itself as very nurturing and supportive. A good feeling and generally upbeat vibe permeated the office, until at one point the company said, "We're here to do business; you've got to take care of yourselves." It was very strange and unsettling to navigate a culture of meaningful work as one big, happy family, and then suddenly lose that support. Like many others, I had been lulled into a sense of comfort, and when the ball dropped, I thought, "What do you mean, you're not looking out for me?"

We have to take responsibility for ourselves, but we don't have to take responsibility *by* ourselves. Next up, we'll be taking a close look at the values of connection, commitment, and resiliency.

CHAPTER 2

INVEST IN YOURSELF

People can't live with change if there's not a changeless core inside them. The key to the ability to change is a changeless sense of who you are, what you are about and what you value.[1]

—STEPHEN COVEY

Before you start to cultivate new skills for the future of work, you need to have a strong sense of what you stand for, who you stand with, and what you want your contribution to be to the world. Your professional development can only go as far as your own personal development. Success rests on investing in the fundamentals of values, connection, and commitment to stay grounded and resilient in the face of accelerating change.

1 Steven R. Covey, *The 7 Habits of Highly Effective People: Powerful Lessons in Personal Change* (New York: Simon & Schuster, 2013).

VALUES INVESTING

Warren Buffet popularized the term "value investing" when he encouraged prioritizing investing in companies with intrinsic value over those the market had overvalued through trends or publicity. Although not particularly sexy, value investing is a pragmatic and lucrative approach. I use the term "values investing" (with an "s") to describe investing in the foundational self-awareness, environment, and network that can help each of us anchor ourselves in our new world of work.

So what do I mean by values? These are our convictions about what we believe is important and desirable. These are the key values that stay steadfast regardless of changes in the market or fads. Values cut across our projects and personal lives, help us make better decisions, prioritize, and remain true to our most deeply-held beliefs. They help us resist the lure of immediate gratification, social pressures, and short-term urgency. Combining these with a strong network and good sense of our strengths and contribution gives us an identity and rootedness beyond our job title.

STRATEGY IS HOW YOU SPEND YOUR TIME

When I cleared my starry eyes and left the glorious, high-flying, airport lounge world of the road warrior, understanding what was important in my life and then making that a priority anchored me. At the office, I valued the work ethic and teamwork that allowed my coworkers and I to consistently meet or exceed targets. I felt pretty sure that I knew my values but would have had a hard time articulating them if asked. The nagging feeling that I was unfulfilled also made me question what aspects I was missing. One day I asked, "What would it look like if I invested as much time and effort into the life I want and the person I want to become as I do into the ideas, ambitious targets, and relationships at work?" Strategy is where you spend your time, and I knew that I wasn't spending the right kind of time creating a sustainable, successful life for myself.

Reflecting to clarify what was important was useful. I put in a lot of time considering and reflecting on what priorities, when satisfied, gave me my own version of "the good life." These included learning and personal growth; contributing to family and, more broadly, future generations; and autonomy and entrepreneurial spirit. While these may sound like values anyone would have, other values that are also attractive like creativity, balance, wealth, or job security are things I am willing to sacrifice for my higher values. I'll admit, too, that these values have changed over time. Starting out, I would have ranked adventure and financial independence (the "can pay my rent on a shared studio in New York" kind versus not having to work). The essence of my values hasn't changed, but the focus certainly has. At any stage of my life, a nice stable job in a rigidly structured company, for example, would kill me. My father, when asked what legacy he wanted to leave his grandchildren, said, "being an outsider." This might be perceived by some as a negative trait, but he meant it as a call to intelligently question the status quo. These are some of the values you might find yourself considering as you think about what matters to you and in what order of priority.

Why do we need to reflect and nurture our values to navigate the work world? We know a tree must have a strong trunk to spread its branches wide. In terms of values investing, we need strong cores as well. The best long-term business investments you can make are in companies with high intrinsic value, and the best investment you can make in yourself is to get in touch with your own intrinsic values.

KNOWING YOUR CORE VALUES

When I was in business school, ethics had not yet become a widely taught subject outside of the philosophy department. Now, most business programs teach ethics because of the issues born of the Enron and financial crises. Going beyond crisis to opportunity, Paul Ingram, Kravis Professor of Business at Columbia Business School, leads a course in the MBA program focused on discovering and understanding your values. The course helps students achieve a sense of self-awareness regarding their personality, needs, habits, and emotions, and teaches them how to leverage these traits to develop better decision-making skills. This isn't just a "nice to have"; Ingram's research has shown that "the alignment of your top values with your job explains 25 percent of job satisfaction. In the US economy, about 2.5 percent of job satisfaction is explained by what people are paid. So you could say values are ten times more important than pay."[2]

Considering our priorities and values and reflecting on them is powerful. This is partly because they often develop from our family or our faith, and we don't question them. We don't think about where they come from, or whether or not we agree with them.

Dr. Jane Horan has studied career transitions for over two decades and notes, "If you're disconnected from your core values, there is dissonance, and feelings of emptiness. Some of us fall into our career rather than taking an active role. We may also subscribe to others' wants and needs rather than our own."[3]

---

2 The Financial Times, "Putting a Price on Principles," *Columbia Business School*, October 4, 2018, accessed October 10, 2018, https://www8.gsb.columbia.edu/articles/ideas-work/putting-price-principles.

3 Jane Horan, *Now It's Clear: The Career You Own*, (UK: Springtime, 2018).

If we don't understand our core values, we'll execute in a disconnected way. A more informed mindset gives us a solid foundation, so when we do innovate and fail, we have a strong sense of values to come back to. As leadership experts Jim Kouzes and Barry Posner say in their seminal book *The Leadership Challenge*, "Values influence every aspect of our lives: our moral judgments, our responses to others, our commitments to personal and organizational goals."[4]

What drives you in a situation? Is it teamwork? The thrill of adventure? Is it learning or curiosity? Knowing your core values leads to greater self-awareness and more enlightened decision-making and helps you understand your motivations. Investing in self-awareness, which some research says diminishes with power and experience, can in turn help you be more confident, creative, and productive.

How do you figure out what your values are? Think about a situation you're dealing with at work and try to understand it in relation to values. One of my values is investing in future generations. Positively expressed, this means that I spend time on people's professional and personal development at work and via coaching entrepreneurs and nonprofit leaders. However, the negative side of this is

---

4 James M. Kouzes and Barry Z. Posner, *The Leadership Challenge: How to Make Extraordinary Things Happen in Organizations*, 6th (Hoboken: Wiley, 2017).

that I catch myself being unhappy when someone doesn't want what is taken as overbearing advice. Think of a time when you were particularly angry or happy with something, and you are likely to find your values. Labeling what and why things are important to you and prioritizing them is a simple and very beneficial exercise.

If you prefer to go more in depth, Kouzes and Posner pioneered one set of values and the process by which you can sort these into your most important ones. There are now many lists of possible values (I've listed a few on the Future Proof website to get you started). Dr. Jane Horan has a workbook I like, *Now It's Clear: The Career You Own*, to help people understand their values, strengths, and purpose.[5] Even if you have done the exercise before as part of a leadership team or coaching, it is worth coming back to regularly and looking through to see how your values can relate to future opportunities.

We often hear from people or say ourselves that success feels hollow despite achievement, titles, remuneration, and recognition. We complain about being bored or stifled, but we don't talk about it because it would be unseemly given the problems others face in the world. These talents and skills could be put to more engaged use. What if the resources poured into obtaining past suc-

---

5 Jane Horan, *Now It's Clear.*

cess could be used to invest in something more important to us?

The world is full of problems to solve. Understanding what's most important to you is a simple first step that not many people take time to appreciate on a regular basis. Take a moment to stop and write down what values will guide you in your shift from hollow success to significance and meaning.

PRACTICING VALUES AND PURPOSE

Although it is popular now for people to talk about purpose as a moment of divine calling, purpose and commitment are more of a practice than a destination—a practice of finding opportunities related to our values where we can contribute.

One pivotal moment in my career, and my life, occurred when I worked with groups of secondary students through a nonprofit business chamber. I invited students from low-income neighborhoods to come to our office. It was an opportunity for them to learn from someone with whom they wouldn't typically come in contact. Many of them had never been to the central business district. They sat in our skyscraper's boardroom, fidgeting in their stiff school uniforms, taking in the gorgeous view of the harbor.

One day, we had twelve students come into the office. After our chat, I asked them about their education, and they said, "We feel like we study for an exam we will never pass." Sadly, this is true. Historically, only 18 percent of Hong Kong students pass the main exam to get subsidized university schooling. The statistics are worse in particularly troubled neighborhoods. The children said, "We don't even know what's out there because all we're good at after four years is taking a test, and we're not really good at that either."

I found others were similarly concerned about helping future generations navigate the future of work, and together, we launched the Opportunity Festival for Creativity, Entrepreneurship, and Innovation. Hundreds of students attended, and corporate executives, NGOs, and entrepreneurs from many different organizations told their stories or brought in maker-like experiences for students to try. Tesla drove a car onto the school's basketball court and placed it next to the helicopter engine where China Aircraft Leasing was introducing students to learning how to fly a helicopter and identify engine parts. We had drone racing, and an MIT Innovation Node provided molecular gastronomy labs. Otis Elevator had virtual reality elevators of the world and a workshop showing kids how to make their own rope-and-pulley elevators. It was a crazy, fun festival that helped connect students to internships and opportunities, allowing them to get out in the world and uncover their passions.

A similar story of turning values into opportunities is Leong Cheung. Cheung used to work demanding hours for private equity firm Bain Capital. At one point in his life, he decided to start focusing on his health and started running, working up to running multiple marathons. He was excited to share his enthusiasm with others and, ultimately, decided to leave Bain Capital and start a nonprofit called RunOurCity.

RunOurCity offers running programs to young kids in low-income areas. The programs pair participants with executives and volunteers who are passionate about running. They use running to teach kids how to set goals, keep a routine, push through adversity, and do their best. RunOurCity uses running as a metaphor for motivation and success, while connecting people in a shared, healthy activity.

This is a powerful example of accomplishing something by gathering people around you and inspiring commitment. Once you realize the potential, you're motivated to prioritize your time and commit the resources you need to achieve the goal. It, and other volunteer work, also led Cheung to being approached by the Hong Kong Jockey Club, one of the world's top ten charitable foundations by giving. He is now head of charities there with a whole new chapter ahead of him.

Many people have a passion that is directly impact related. They volunteer, or they have a huge passion to make something better in the world, which can become the basis for a second career. It's a spark for tremendous energy and excitement that combines to make a more energized and flexible person. Connecting with others around your shared values often leads to opportunities to contribute and build a network of support.

FORTIFYING FOR A NEW WORLD OF WORK

Connection is one of the most rewarding investments for fortifying ourselves in today's volatile and rapidly changing work environment. We shouldn't take human connection for granted on a professional or personal level. Many people simply fail to remember to invest in important people in their lives because they're too busy. As David Mattin, Global Head of Trends at TrendWatching says, "Modernity has atomized us, tearing apart the traditional bonds of family and friendship in pursuit of constant productivity and economic growth. In the 21st century, automation and AI will both obviate the need for much human labour and create conditions of even greater and more disorientating change. The practical conditions are in place for a turn back to one another."[6]

6 David Mattin, "Stop Waiting for the Singularity. It Started 200 Years Ago," *NewCo Shift*, March 7, 2018, accessed September 30, 2018, https://shift.newco.co/2018/03/07/Stop-Waiting-for-the-Singularity--It-Started-200-Years-Ago.

In the past, there was a reliable structure provided by neighborhoods, churches, and our families. These environments offered a sense of belonging and connection because we were all in the same place. Many members of my family still live in the same town, as do the majority of my high school alumni. Work itself has provided a structure for relationships and water cooler conversation.

But today, people often are widely dispersed, and they travel for work or move to where the jobs are. Even when they are physically near each other, they're connecting virtually on social media. People sit in bed at night, texting their spouse in the next room about what's happening the next day. Susan Bird, TED Fellow and CEO of global consultancy wf360, which promotes the art and importance of conversation, calls the advent of texting, "birth control for conversations."[7]

Kate Otto, author of *Everyday Ambassador* and currently a physician working to improve health outcomes and build communities around the world, sees this as a "disconnectivity paradox," or the notion that the more digitally connected we become, the more emotionally disconnected we end up from one another. As a young person backpacking around the world, she realized that with the increase in technology, we can't take offline, face-to-face connection for granted. We need to put our phones down

7 Susan Bird (connection), interviewed by Diana Wu David of Future Proof.

and genuinely connect with the important people in our lives, and those we've just met. Kate noted the invigorating experience of making connections with people on her trips, getting outside of her comfort zone, and developing the empathy, patience, and humility to connect. "Human relationships are at the center of making a positive difference in the world. Meaningful human connection is hard work, but it is essential to your career, to your development, and I think to the survival of our society."[8]

WE ALL NEED 3:00 A.M. FRIENDS

Connecting isn't always easy. Former US Surgeon General, Vivek Murthy, wrote in *Harvard Business Review* that, "we live in the most technologically connected age in the history of civilization, yet rates of loneliness have doubled since the 1980s," and predicts this as the next big healthcare epidemic.[9] We are all so connected by technology, yet many feel alone in this crowded world. To flourish, we need to invest in connections with others that are real beyond the persona we project at work or in social media.

I've thought a lot about this, largely due to the consequences of my friend's suicide. Certainly, we could text

---

8 Kate Otto (connection), interviewed by Diana Wu David of Future Proof, July 18, 2017.

9 Vivek Murthy, "Work and the Loneliness Epidemic," *Harvard Business Review*, September 2017, accessed September 30, 2018, https://hbr.org/cover-story/2017/09/work-and-the-loneliness-epidemic.

and talk whenever we wanted to, but that moment of losing Charlotte made me realize that more than ever in this globalized, disconnected, changeable world, we need personal connections, people I call my "3 a.m. friends."

A core network of support, 3 a.m. friends are the people you can call in the middle of the night who will drop everything for you and help in your moment of need. I've had moments in the past where I was so upset that I literally walked out of my apartment in gym shorts with no money, crying, and called a close friend to say, "I just need to talk." She said, "Tell me where you are. I'm dropping everything and we're going to go get a drink!" It didn't matter what she was doing at the time, because our relationship in that moment was most important and she knew I needed her. We ended up sitting outside on the lawn near my apartment. I don't even remember what we talked about, but it was so important to know that she was out there.

There was nobody Charlotte could call at three o'clock in the morning who could come to her to intervene in a bad situation. My own long-distance let-down as a friend made me realize that there is an element of personal face-to-face connection that needs to be present in our lives. When dear friends have moved away, I know I'll need to have someone to take me out for that drink. It's amazing that you can find a tribe of like-minded people anywhere in the world with just an internet connection, yet so many of us fail to invest in and connect personally with the people we can rely on for deeper support when life throws us a grenade.

Unfortunately, when we optimize for efficiency or "likes" over human connection, those relationships suffer.

STRENGTH IN COMMUNITY: FINDING YOUR TRIBE

Much like the tribes of the olden days, community involves connection to place, routines, purpose, and working together to find solutions. Connected communities allow people to weather the emotional ups and downs of work and life, and to gain energy and inspiration in a less-structured environment. We can learn how to maintain our sense of belonging despite the transient reality of today's modern world by taking a lesson from the nomadic tribes that have managed to exist for centuries.

In 2016, I went to Mongolia with Anthony Willoughby and Josie Stoker, who started the Nomadic Business School and have been visiting nomadic tribes across Asia and Africa to study how they've been able to maintain purpose, clarity, and agility over time. We stayed with a family in the Altai Mountains, camping around their yurt and using their horses and camels to explore the surrounding plains. The elder of the family, whom we called Ata, showed us tools they have used for generations. "This tent pole is from my great-grandfather and this is how we've managed to organize ourselves over time, where every season we must move, and we face great adversity," he told us. It was fascinating to learn how these people survived for so long. It certainly made me wonder what my own equivalent tent pole might be.

In today's world, we are continuing to find our own tribes. As Seth Godin, the wildly successful business executive, blogger, and author, discussed in his TED talk, "the internet has ended mass marketing and revived the anthropological human social unit of the distant past, which is tribes. It's founded on shared ideas and values and it gives ordinary people the power to lead and make a big change."[10] This concept is becoming even more fitting for the age we live in.

Anthony and his group talked to many different tribes to understand how some of the old ways can be transformed into the modern way we work. He says it's about the connections that give us "airbags of trust" so that whatever happens, we can bounce back.[11] Traditional societies are models for groups that form together around a commit-

---

10 Seth Godin. (2009). *The Tribes We Lead* [Video]. Retrieved September 30, 2018 from https://www.ted.com/talks/seth_godin_on_the_tribes_we_lead?language=en.

11 Anthony Willoughby (connections), interviewed by Diana Wu David of Future Proof, August 2018.

ment, a purpose, or a community. This is becoming more essential to our work lives today.

Think about what tribes you might belong to. Nurture them to develop a network of connections around your interests and values, and to understand yourself more in the context of community.

Shveitta Sharma, Chief Happiness Officer at the School of Happiness, works with Google and other companies on interpersonal relationships and enhancing teams. Shveitta often talks about the connections we make, comparing them to the giant California redwoods.[12] The trees are hundreds of feet tall and live an average of 500 years. One would imagine they have roots that connect deep into the ground to support those majestic branches. The reality, however, is that their roots extend only six to eight feet. Their real strength is that they grow in clusters and use their network to support each other. When one of them gets "sick," the others compensate by sending their nutrients to the affected tree. They all hold each other up, which is a beautiful metaphor for community and resilience in our own lives.

12 Shveitta Sethi Sharma. (2014). *The Secret to Being Happy* [Video]. Retrieved September 30, 2018 from https://www.youtube.com/watch?v=oQ6EEYoxSpQ.

POSITIVE CONNECTION BUILDS THE WORLD

How does this relate to our work in an age of accelerating change? First, according to a whitepaper by Cognizant, a consulting company analyzing the future of work, innately human abilities like connection, caring, and coaching have been identified as the main common themes among the top twenty-one jobs of the future.[13] As algorithms take over, we humans need to specialize in the things a computer can't do better than us. Second, the ability to invest in and gain from a strong network of connections is a key aspect that senior leaders feel is important to the success of their teams. CEOs have asked me to come in and talk about the importance of connection and resilience in weathering a volatile and unpredictable market. In these moments, we need to pull together, rather than close down.

Do you have people you can call upon to help you when you need to take a project over the line and need a huge favor beyond the call of duty? Do you have people you can call to help you through bad times? People who know you and respect you beyond how useful you are or your social media presence? Do you know who makes up your tribe or tribes? That network gives you roots and a strong core.

---

13 Ben Pring, Robert H. Brown, Euan Davis, Manish Bahl, and Michael Cook, "21 Jobs of the Future: A Guide to Getting—and Staying—Employed Over the Next Ten Years," *Cognizant*, https://www.cognizant.com/whitepapers/21-jobs-of-the-future-a-guide-to-getting-and-staying-employed-over-the-next-10-years-codex3049.pdf.

Finally, this positive connection can help us build a more inclusive and resilient society and creates new opportunities. For example, the value of connection is at the heart of Brian Tang's Young Makers & ChangeMakers social enterprise. Originally created to provide his own son with opportunities in maker education that Tang saw available elsewhere around the world but lacking in Hong Kong, inclusion was always a focus to ensure that youth in the community had access to such important mindsets and skills for the digital economy regardless of gender, ethnicity, or socio-economic background. At the same time, the platform connects youth from all backgrounds to allow them to better learn and appreciate their different values and individual abilities.

CONNECTION FOSTERS RESILIENCE

Investing in connection and in our sense of purpose lays a foundation of resilience, a concept that's often overlooked but crucial in a volatile, uncertain world. Nassim Taleb, the author of *The Black Swan*, which explained the increase of unpredictable events such as the financial crisis, says in order to compete, people and companies need to take the concept of resilience to the next level.[14] In his book, *Antifragile*, he said, "Antifragility is beyond resilience or robustness. The resilient resists shocks and

14 Nassim Nicholas Taleb, *The Black Swan: The Impact of the Highly Improbable*, 2nd (New York: Random House, 2010).

stays the same. The antifragile gets better."[15] Antifragility isn't just a restorative bounce, but a way of approaching life in an ongoing way to learn from our mistakes; not just bouncing back but bouncing forward and framing our experiences as a catalyst for growth.

For instance, as a young girl, Shveitta lived with her family at an army base in India where her father was a high-ranking officer. When army staff received new postings, a colorfully-painted train laden with flowers rolled into the base to transfer them to a new location, with all the staff and crew waving them off in a big celebration. As the day drew near for them to leave, she waited for the flower train to come and bring her family to their next adventure. Sadly, her father passed away a week before her ninth birthday and from there, her life took a dramatic turn. Shveitta's mother took her and her little brother to live with her mother's parents, who were quite strict and not demonstrative with love. She changed schools mid-term and children ostracized her as a newcomer.

This motivated her to study how we can make meaningful connections, even under the worst circumstances. She says, "I think resilience develops as a means of survival. Going through pain and coming out on the other side makes you realize that one can survive anything. Every

---

15 Nassim Nicholas Taleb, *Antifragile: Things That Gain from Disorder* (New York: Random House, 2012).

time I experience a setback, I recall all the tough times I have faced and I put things in perspective and realize that if I could overcome that I most certainly can overcome what's next."[16] She has come to value the experience as a catalyst for her life's work, helping people lead meaningful lives of resilience and connection.

We don't learn resilience in school and we don't cultivate it enough by investing in our health, vitality, and relationships. We don't think about it much at all until things go bad, but we can seek out opportunities to enhance resilience. As Facebook COO, Sheryl Sandberg writes in *Option B*, when she lost her husband, she realized resiliency isn't something we're born with.[17] We don't get a fixed amount of resilience. It's a muscle we can exercise and strengthen through challenges. We can seek out these tests to become someone who not only bounces back from adversity, but someone who gains from it.

How do we build our resilience muscle? We exercise it. University of Nebraska psychologist Dr. Richard Dienstbier developed a toughness model after studying the neurological connections that affect how people respond to adversity. He found that people who had built up a

---

16 Shveitta Sharma (resilience) interviewed by Diana Wu David of Future Proof, September 23, 2018.

17 Sheryl Sandberg and Adam Grant, *Option B: Facing Adversity, Building Resilience, and Finding Joy* (New York: Knopf, 2017).

toughness could respond to adversity. They also tend to take it a step further by seeking new opportunities to test and challenge themselves.[18] Like a broken bone that becomes stronger when it heals, people have the capacity to use adversity as stimulation to pick themselves up and grow.

Investing in ourselves for a good foundation and investing in our connections and sense of purpose are important, but capitalizing on adversity and moving forward to understand how we can pivot and learn gives us a tremendous advantage. It allows us to think about things more broadly and opportunistically, focusing not only on ourselves, but about how we connect to others. Commitment, connection, and resiliency come together to allow us to build a flexible life with a strong core and take advantage of many opportunities, go in different directions, and grow in varied ways over a longer lifespan.

In the next section, we'll discuss some of the practices we can develop to build on this solid foundation. We'll also dive deeper into additional skills that create value and resiliency relevant to our situation.

18 Meg Jay, "The Secrets of Resilience," *The Wall Street Journal*, November 10, 2017, accessed September 30, 2018, https://www.wsj.com/articles/the-secrets-of-resilience-1510329202.

PART II

CULTIVATE: THE VIRTUES TO STAY ENGAGED AND RELEVANT

If you don't like change, you're going to like irrelevance even less.

—GENERAL ERIC SHINSEKI

Experiential learning—learning by doing, versus learning by any other method such as reading or observing—is integral to cultivating the virtues and mastering key skills to make the most of the new world of work. Part II, *Cultivate*, focuses on actionable opportunities for experiential learning.

CHAPTER 3

EXPERIMENT

Endless innovation for its own sake is unproductive but you can understand who you are at your best; explore experimentation; and discover the purpose of work beyond financial rewards.[1]

—DANIEL CABLE, ORGANIZATION PSYCHOLOGIST

Experimentation is essential to innovation and goes hand-in-hand with an entrepreneurial mindset. Businesses are facing challenges they often don't see coming, and they are asking their people to be willing to experiment and adopt an entrepreneurial mindset.

We also need to adapt our own careers. Reid Hoffman, founder of LinkedIn, encourages us "to rediscover our

1 Emma Jacobs, "How to Unleash Your Dormant Enthusiasm for Work," *Financial Times*, March 18, 2018, accessed September 20, 2018, https://www.ft.com/content/e1fe96a8-26d4-11e8-b27e-cc62a39d57a0.

entrepreneurial instincts and use them to forge new sorts of careers. Whether you're a lawyer or doctor or teacher or engineer or even a business owner, today you need to also think of yourself as an entrepreneur at the helm of at least one living, growing start-up venture: your career."[2]

The Dilbert comic strip parodies innovation and leadership in its characterization of the buzzword-happy boss talking about change—as long as it's everybody else that's changing. In reality, most leaders have had to experiment with and adapt their business, their products, and their own leadership style. Adopting an experimental and open mindset frees us to discover the creative solutions at work that everyone needs in today's complex world.

EXPERIMENT WITH THE TOOLS YOU HAVE

In the past, we referred to the process of innovation as "trial and error." We now call it innovation. Whether in a startup, a government brochure, or a large organization, innovation is trendy. Though CEOs may go so far as to mandate it, many companies aren't built to support it, are not clear on their desired outcomes, and their leadership is unwilling to make the necessary changes to the current structure to facilitate success.

I was invited to speak at a large bank that had adopted

2 Reid Hoffman and Ben Casnocha, *The Start-Up of You*, 3.

entrepreneurial branding to service the company's many wealthy new business tycoons; the brief was to have everyone "think entrepreneurial" without quitting their jobs. I recognized the irony, but in fact, all entrepreneurs have constraints, and being entrepreneurial within a corporation is just another set of pros and cons. It is up to us to experiment within existing parameters in both our professional and personal lives. We can all do better when we adopt an open mindset that uses experiments as opportunities for learning. To borrow the words of BCG Henderson Institute's Martin Reeves on adaptive companies, our goal should be to "generate, test, and replicate a larger number of innovative ideas faster, at lower cost, and with less risk than our rivals."[3]

The head of marketing at *Financial Times* in Asia, Nashua Gallagher, provides another example of how small changes, built upon over time, lead to new avenues for professional and personal growth. When she was young, Nashua got involved in the poetry scene, where she discovered her tribe. As she climbed the ladder in her professional career, she found that poetry was a great opportunity to practice and expand her creativity. Creating imagery with words improved her marketing skills, and the poetry scene provided her with access to

3 Martin Reeves and Mike Deimler, "Adaptability: The New Competitive Advantage," *Harvard Business Review*, July-August 2011, accessed September 30, 2018, https://hbr.org/2011/07/adaptability-the-new-competitive-advantage.

a wider variety of people. Instead of collaborating only with people who talked about digital marketing and search engine optimization, Nashua spent evenings talking about ways to conceptualize grief or express it in a verbal image. Poetry dramatically enriched the way she approached problems, and she recently published a book of poems.

Nashua has also started hosting creativity workshops in corporate settings and talking in schools about how to embrace creativity to enhance life. She melds community with creativity to invest in and connect with a tribe. For Nashua, it's an experiment that has brought fulfillment, a reputation beyond her job role, and further added value to her corporate job.

In his book *Originals: How Nonconformists Move the World,* Adam Grant, a social scientist at the Wharton School of Business, talks about experiments as a way to separate "idea doubt" and "self-doubt."[4] Nashua can have a bad poem without destroying her self-esteem if she learns from it and gets up the next day to try again. Entrepreneurs go through the experimental process often. However, people in structured environments, such as traditional corporations, aren't always used to experimenting and failing. The process is a useful opportunity to develop new ideas, learn lessons, and strengthen resiliency.

4 Adam Grant, *Originals: How Nonconformists Move the World* (New York: Penguin, 2017).

Thomas Edison said trying without success is not failure, you've just found the first several thousand things that won't work. When a failed experiment gives me a sense of deep personal failure, I'm learning to embrace failure as feedback on the method, product, or idea and capture the knowledge for future projects.

FAIL FAST, FAIL FORWARD

There's an entire language built around "failing fast, failing forward." If we can be curious about why an experiment didn't work, we can take advantage of those opportunities to learn.

Recovering from failure is easier if you have a broad agenda and take small steps. Nashua's idea of embracing poetry began as a visit to a poetry reading and was a way to satisfy her need for community and creativity. Pursuing something that interests you and seeking to learn more about it is personally enriching. It opens a new aspect of your identity beyond job title or function. Learning something new each year will also keep your brain fit. Martin Lau is the president of Tencent in China, one of the largest internet companies in the world. Speaking at an education summit, he said, "Learning to learn is the key to success. It's the deal breaker. It's the one thing you need to have."[5]

5 Martin Lau, Yidan Summit, December 10, 2017.

Technologist and founding editor of *Wired* Kevin Kelly talks about the importance of learning to learn, or meta-learning, as a key competitive advantage. Rather than finding the next big thing, he says, "Master the art of learning quickly."[6] Iterate and experiment quickly. Generating tests and replicating a large number of innovative ideas faster, at lower cost and less risk, than anyone else is an ability that crosses industry boundaries.

Indeed, experimenting is a way to learn *and* it's a way to learn how we learn things. Having discrete trials to develop specific abilities, such as creating imagery and writing poetry, develops the process by which we know and understand how to learn.

This can apply to *how* we work—tools, environments, routines, collaborations—as well as what we work *on*. Leadership expert, Tara Mohr, calls this tuning your instrument.[7] JJ Acuna, a talented artist and architect, calls this concept "finding the right tools to paint your life."[8]

If you tried the small brush and that didn't work, maybe

---

6 Kevin Kelly, *The Inevitable: Understanding the 12 Technological Forces That Will Shape Our Future* (New York: Penguin, 2017).

7 Tara Mohr, "You Are the Instrument of Your Work, *TaraMohr.com*, accessed October 10, 2018, https://www.taramohr.com/tools-and-inspiration-for-playing-bigger/you-are-the-instrument.

8 JJ Acuna, "What Is Your Life's Purpose?" panel hosted by The Busy Woman Project, February 8, 2018, Hong Kong.

you need a roller. What colors should *you* use? What canvas and paint? This imagery has always stayed with me, applied in different situations. Consider your canvas. Do you need a dedicated workspace, or can you work from anywhere? Do you want to lead a team or work independently? Is working eighty-hour weeks exciting or draining? What works for you may not work for someone else, and that's fine. Your canvas, and your painting, is a personal choice that should be created to fit your life. LinkedIn's Reid Hoffman, in a computer analogy, calls this *permanent beta*, which "forces you to acknowledge that you have bugs, that there's new development to do on yourself, that you will need to adapt and evolve." That need for constant improvement can be intimidating but is nonetheless an optimistic view that empowers you to improve yourself and the world around you.[9]

Taking small, active steps to develop specific abilities and reflecting on these "micro actions" develops the process by which we understand how *we* learn as opposed to anyone else. Lazslo Block, Google's former SVP of People Operations, started Humu, an AI-backed system to nudge us to try, learn, and improve in the workplace.[10] Dr. Tal Ben-Shahar and Angus Ridgway, the partners who started the learning and development company

9 Reid Hoffman and Ben Casnocha, *The Start-up of You*.

10 "Google's former head of HR wants to help people act more human at work." By Jena McGRegor, The Washington Post, October 18, 2018.

Potentialife, noticed that their corporate culture projects weren't successful as top-down ideas. They decided to target new workplace behaviors one by one to develop personal feedback loops enabled by technology. This led to huge cultural shifts, increased engagement, and business results in their clients' organizations.[11] Reflection and action must go hand in hand. We can't learn how to ride a bike by watching videos of it, and we can't "think" our way to leadership. We have to actually practice new behaviors, one by one.

These small steps can lead to big results, especially as technology and the gig economy combine to create ease of experimentation and scale. It used to require a lot of money to even launch a website, but by the mid-nineties I could generate a website from my living room. Now it's possible to start an entire company with freelancers or satellite offices around the world.

MY INVESTMENT EXPERIMENT

In 2014, I was discussing an opportunity to go into a partnership at a venture capital business. It meant lots of work and little immediate income, but less travel and more excitement than my corporate position. The other upside was that I could invest in the company and build some equity for myself. I was excited about the

11 Angus Ridgeway, presentation to American Chamber of Hong Kong, March 16, 2018.

possibilities, but it would have put a strain on the family finances, so I decided to experiment with a phased approach instead.

Rather than quitting my job to become a full-time early stage investor, I kept my job, joined the advisory board of this new company, then allocated a portion of my salary to angel investment so I could start learning what it would be like to invest my own money and fulfill my aim of learning more about the business before making a big and potentially irreversible move.

We crave the earth-shattering move, the "burn the boats," never-turning-back extreme makeover; but day-to-day iterations and trials are often where the magic is.

I worked to define my investment thesis, but realized, in the end, the investment process itself wasn't as interesting to me as the operations and advising companies how to grow and scale. I most liked being at the forefront of ideas and navigating the future, but I found the administrative aspect tedious, despite it being crucial to investment success. The experience was an incredibly helpful learning lesson because it taught me about my strengths and interests, and it helped guide my career choices towards more advisory work and less investment.

EMBRACING EXPERIMENTATION IN OUR CAREERS

Certain minds thrive in uncertain times and adopting an iterative mindset, and experimentation in careers is becoming more common. In this section, I'll show you a few examples to give you some ideas of how you might go forward.

One example is Michelle Paisley, a banker with over twenty-five years of experience in public and private equity markets, with a strong, global track record in sales, investing, research, and leadership. Michelle is interested in inclusive finance and using blockchain technology, the cryptocurrency digital ledger, in ways that it has not previously been used to reduce friction and improve efficiency in the funding-investing cycle. She explored opportunities with potential partners willing to embrace her ideas from crowdfunding to millennial-focused, app-based investing—including a short-term entrepreneur in residence project to see if their assumptions were correct. If they hit certain milestones, she stays on, and if not, she takes what she has learned and tries another avenue.[12] Michelle says, "My goal continues to be to build a new sort of finance institution and I am working with two amazing female partners (with all the regulatory structures in place) and building a network of people doing

12 Michelle Paisley (experimentation), interviewed by Diana Wu David of Future Proof, March 12, 2018.

related innovative activities that I think may in time form part of the bigger picture."[13]

Mohammed Sam Shoushi, a former government affairs specialist at Google, is another example of an executive whose iterative experiments led to a whole new world of work. Sam has a passion for yoga and mindfulness, which he developed on the side of his corporate job. He would go on retreats and continue learning. Google also has a "Search Inside Yourself" class for employees, and there he learned how mindfulness and self-awareness contribute to corporate enhancement, in addition to personal wellbeing. Eventually, he decided to switch it up a little. He didn't want to just be at Google and spend his free time doing mindfulness activities; he wanted to combine mindfulness with his corporate understanding. Now, he works at a company called the Potential Project that coaches corporate clients in the art of mindful leadership. He said, "It's great. It's everything I know from before, but the weight has shifted on the scales to more mindfulness. I've gone over to the other side, and I'm learning it from a totally new perspective."[14]

---

13 Michelle Paisley, October 8, 2018.

14 Mohammed Sam Soushi (experimentation), interviewed by Diana Wu David of Future Proof, June 21, 2018.

THE EXPERIMENTAL MINDSET AT WORK

If your company's structures don't facilitate experimentation, perhaps you've already given up on tapping into your inner entrepreneur. Don't give up. Build a reputation for innovation instead. When new projects come along, you will be one of the first to get pulled into them and that can illuminate ways to recraft your job to include new opportunities. Some companies bring together diverse parties to become innovation ambassadors across departments and functions. Others allow rotations into company innovation labs or accelerators to give a sense of what projects and resources are available and help spread the culture throughout the business. In companies without much focus on innovation, we can try to be a catalyst to bring people together ourselves. Identify potential disruptions or opportunities to take the business further and gather other interested parties to form an internal innovation brain trust.

Trying and failing at experiments makes us internal disruptors before outside competitors can do the same. Clayton Christensen's renowned business reference, *The Innovator's Dilemma*, describes incumbent companies perpetually disrupted by smaller upstarts.[15] This is similar to what we face if we're stagnant in our career or if we've invested heavily in just one specific industry.

---

15 Clayton M. Christensen, *The Innovator's Dilemma: The Revolutionary Book That Will Change the Way You Do Business* (New York: HarperCollins, 2003).

We may be an expert in that field but being able to think widely and strategically allows us to recognize ways to disrupt our habits.

Jennifer Van Dale is an employment lawyer and partner at Eversheds Sutherland, and one of the firm's go-to experts on future-of-work issues. "It started in 2016 when a client wanted preliminary advice on an 'Uber for healthcare' idea, a platform for home healthcare visits. We didn't do the project, but I realized that there is a real risk in this model that our clients weren't thinking about because often these gig workers are classified as employees. There are also licensing issues; healthcare is a very personal service, so you should do personal background checks. You could have people fake needing a physical therapist and picking a cute one. Risks go both ways. The client didn't go through with it, but it started my research and interest in gig workers."[16]

Intrigued by her client's demands on the firm to figure out the messy contractual issues involved in the future of work, Jennifer started thinking about these ideas, blogging about them on LinkedIn, and publishing thought leadership via her firm. Then the American Chamber in Hong Kong found out about her expertise and asked her to do a policy talk on gig workers. She has become a well-known expert and has carved out a niche for

16 Jennifer Van Dale, (gig workers), interviewed by Diana Wu David of Future Proof, May 15, 2018.

herself, combining employment law skills with forward-thinking ideas on work trends. She said, "I couldn't do this twenty-five years ago because I wouldn't have had the experience or credentials, but I am glad that I can pursue new avenues."[17]

A similar situation encouraged new learning for Natalie Da Gama-Rose, chief counsel at Lane Crawford, a high-end luxury retailer based in Asia. The company started an accelerator program, taking on many different suppliers and companies and testing new fashion trends. They were suddenly looking at the potential of being surrounded by an orbit of contracts and share options. Natalie was originally hired to "make sure nothing bad happened." She didn't intend to experiment at work but realized that for things to move efficiently, she had to try out fresh ideas to set up the company for a new way of working.

Finally, external societal challenges can inspire innovation. We face myriad external challenges today that we can only hope to solve by collectively focusing our efforts.

For example, Unreasonable Group, a global network and investment firm, partners with emerging leaders from companies like Disney, Pearson, and Barclays, presenting social problems they could solve with existing business

17 Jennifer Van Dale, 2018.

resources. An emerging leader at Barclays discovered that military veterans were not getting loans because they had poor credit. Yet those who did receive loans were very good at repaying. That realization was an opportunity to serve a disenfranchised market by reviewing and changing the way they computed credit scores for veterans. It was a great way to develop a new product to service a new market and expand their lending options.[18]

In all of these cases, executives recognized the potential business needs or issues in their industries and have begun gathering collaborators to develop experiments and novel solutions.

EXPERIMENTATION TAKEAWAYS

Don't underestimate the ability to earn big gains by starting small or taking risks at the edge to understand where you might want to go and learn. Professor Rita McGrath of Columbia Business School, an expert in strategy and entrepreneurship, is a big proponent of learning via failing fast and failing forward. In her research across 5,000 companies, she discovered those that free up resources to invest in nimble "transient advantages" have a unique ability to outperform over time.[19] Learning from error,

18 Anthony Davies, CEO, Barclays Hong Kong panel at Shared Value Forum, Sept 21, 2017.

19 Rita Gunther McGrath, "Continuous Reconfiguration in the Transient Advantage Economy," *Strategy & Leadership*, Vol. 41 Iss: 5, 2013, pp. 17-22.

growing in knowledge, and overcoming challenges to stay ahead applies to you in your career as well. When there's technological or market uncertainty, McGrath likens risks taken and challenges faced to investments in our lives and careers. We don't want to just do nothing and leave ourselves without options. Instead, we can create stepping stones that can lead to new avenues of opportunity.

Another key experimentation takeaway is the feedback loop. Instead of leaning on a "build it and they will come" attitude, test working with new people, projects, or departments. See what is and isn't working against current resources and constraints, and then create a practice and process to do things in the best way possible.

Be bold and experiment at work. It's common to hear from clients, your team, or in the company's annual report to be more entrepreneurial. That's where knowing your own and other's values come in. When I talk to chief innovation officers, success boils down to creating a sense of safety and incentive, be it vision and story or professional or monetary incentive. People are typically hesitant to experiment at work. If you are a leader, think about your role in building safety for others to encourage the experimental and entrepreneurial mindset in your people.

EXERCISES AND ACTION STEPS

There are a variety of strategic ways to take action with experimentation, from learning new skills to identifying external problems.

Do some homework about your current industry or one that has always intrigued you, the challenges it faces, and what others are doing to tackle the obstacles. Identify existing strategic gaps you feel you have in your toolbox such as public speaking or board work that you think would be more broadly interesting realms in which to experiment.

START SMALL AND ACTIONABLE

Develop an annual professional or personal learning goal to keep you fresh. Every year, consider something new you can try to learn and grow. Take a leadership position on a new project at work or a lesser role in something completely new, participate in a professional organization, volunteer, or do a TED talk.

Read books and online articles; Amazon.com is the largest search engine after Google and Facebook and has loads of opportunities to explore.[20]

---

20 Dave Davies, "Meet the 7 Most Popular Search Engines in the World," *Search Engine Journal*, January 7, 2018, accessed November 14, 2018, https://www.searchenginejournal.com/seo-101/meet-search-engines.

Take a class. Between LinkedIn, Coursera, Udemy, Khan Academy, and NovoEd, you can take a class in virtually anything; there is even a Learn How to Learn course. If you are keen to understand what credentials might be useful in future projects, ask someone in that area for a course recommendation.

BUILD A PRACTICE

A single experiment doesn't make you a rock star, but finding a successful practice that works for you and that you can build upon consistently does set you up for success.

Tune your instrument. Work on an attribute, such as being more prepared or being more collaborative. Identify one very concrete, actionable step you can take to grow that skill. Write it down, set a goal for yourself, implement and then reflect on its results to see how you can take the next action step. Those small, iterative aspects are important, especially when you take the time to integrate feedback on how something worked or didn't work, and how you can modify your choices going forward. If you want to get more extreme, google "lifehacking" and see the many interesting experiments you can try.

PRACTICE GETTING OUT OF YOUR COMFORT ZONE

Do something outside your frame of reference, such as taking a class in a completely new activity like juggling, improv comedy, coding, or coaching. Take a trip outside your comfort zone.

FIND A BIG PROBLEM TO SOLVE

For Amazon CEO Jeff Bezos, the focus is on the future, and he spends much of his time on a medium-term road map.[21] What's coming down the line to disrupt your environment or customers? Better yet, have a look at the United Nations Sustainable Development Goals, find one that fits well with your values, and consider how you can use your professional or personal resources to help solve it.

BUILD A NETWORK OF OTHER INNOVATORS

Start connecting and expanding your network. Involve others in your experiments, especially people you traditionally may not consider. Invite them to brainstorming sessions. Maybe your customer renewal rate is abysmally low or millennials are flooding out of your associate pro-

---

21 Steve Denning, "The Seven Things a Highly Agile CEO Does: Jeff Bezos," *Forbes*, September 17, 2018, accessed November 14, 2018, https://www.forbes.com/sites/stevedenning/2018/09/17/the-seven-things-a-highly-agile-ceo-does-jeff-bezos/#7d99cbfb4f09.

gram. Maybe there are some interesting startups with whom you could collaborate. Who might have the greatest insight as to why this issue exists? Gather a group to discuss methods of obtaining information and discuss ideas for solving the problems.

Visit my website www.dianawudavid.com/futureproofinsider for more information, worksheets, and resources.

CHAPTER 4

REINVENT

Human beings are works in progress that constantly think they're finished.[1]

—DAN GILBERT

While you will always be experimenting at the margins and incorporating the feedback you get from it, if you plan to make bigger changes, you may have to prepare to reinvent yourself. Reinvention is a big, intimidating, and trendy topic. Plug "reinvent" into an Amazon search and you will get over 700 responses—granted, some of them will be for makeup or synthetic biology, but you get the picture.

Reinvention is less about the extreme makeover than how to dynamically take advantage of inevitable shifts in your

1 Gilbert, D. (2014). *The Psychology of Your Future Self* [Video]. Retrieved September 29, 2018 from https://www.ted.com/talks/dan_gilbert_you_are_always_changing/transcript.

industry or function. The odds are good that you'll outlast your job, so you have to become comfortable with the process of reinvention and cultivating resilience. Given today's acceleration of change, movement within the workplace relies on the ability to adapt. As South-Africa-based coach Simon Kozlowski puts it, "Reinvention is not a nice-to-have; it's a must-have in how we consider new work, new abilities to learn, and adaptability for long-term success."[2]

This requires some serious flexibility or at least the beginnings of an adaptive blueprint. Leadership pioneer Warren Bennis said, "People who cannot invent and reinvent themselves must be content with borrowed posture, secondhand ideas, and fitting in instead of standing out."[3] This idea has evolved into "the new Q."

WHAT'S YOUR AQ?

IQ and EQ, intelligence quotient and emotional intelligence, have always been hallmarks of success in the past. The third success trait is what Silicon Valley Bank VP Natalie Fratto, calls "AQ," the adaptability quotient.[4] You

2 Simon Kozlowski (reinvention), interviewed by Diana Wu David of Future Proof, April 10, 2018.

3 Warren Bennis (author) and Patricia Ward Biederman (contributor), *The Essential Bennis* (San Francisco: Jossey-Bass, 2009), 5.

4 Natalie Fratto, "Screw Emotional Intelligence–Here's The Key To The Future Of Work," *Fast Company*, January 29, 2018, accessed September 29, 2018 https://www.fastcompany.com/40522394/screw-emotional-intelligence-heres-the-real-key-to-the-future-of-work.

can have intellect and emotional intelligence, but without the ability to adapt you are yesterday's news. In a recent article in *The Guardian*, historian and author Yuval Noah Harari predicted, "Most of what people learn in school or in college will probably be irrelevant by the time they are 40 or 50. If they want to continue to have a job, and to understand the world, and be relevant to what is happening, people will have to reinvent themselves again and again, and faster and faster."[5] Adaptability is the go-to ability for the new age.

You can't book-learn adaptability. Internal entrepreneurship is like working on yourself as if you are your own startup. You must be your own disruptor and interrupter and still be able to thrive. Like it or not, it's inspiring to get knocked on your ass a few times and find the strength to get up, shake it off, and realize you're tough enough to move on.

Many startups run into problems and emotions run high. Several times, the companies that I have worked with floundered for one reason or another: cofounders fell out; product quality failed; a disagreement among key shareholders came to a head, leading to serious disagreements. Each time, it felt like a failure. Yet these were opportuni-

5 Ian Sample, "AI Will Create 'Useless Class' of Human, Predicts Bestselling Historian," *The Guardian*, May 20, 2016, accessed September 29, 2018, https://www.theguardian.com/technology/2016/may/20/silicon-assassins-condemn-humans-life-useless-artificial-intelligence.

ties to put into practice the learning I had done on board behavior, crisis management, or operations. The costs have been the same as my MBA, but the learning is often far greater.

REINVENTION IN ACTION

How do you reinvent your work, either to hedge against obsolescence or because you see an opportunity to move to greener pastures? The best way is to take stock of your assets, strengths, and values and pivot to a niche that is adjacent to or leverages your current expertise.

I worked in consulting with a friend from New York many years ago, and after going our separate ways and having many life experiences, I learned she'd been in a car accident. Confined to a bed for months, she realized she would never be able to do consulting in the same way. Consultants fly every week and work nearly around the clock, and she was simply no longer physically able to handle that lifestyle. Undaunted, my friend analyzed her core skills and attributes and weighed them against opportunity. She knew how to read markets, make connections, and help put people on a good path, and she leveraged that momentum into starting several companies. In her work, she found that roughly 60 percent of startups fail because of poor cofounder communication. With recently honed coaching skills, she launched a company that assists startup cofounders successfully launch their businesses or weather problems.

PROACTIVE REINVENTION: FINDING CHANGE BEFORE IT FINDS YOU

Sometimes reinvention occurs in response to external circumstances, such as a downsizing or technological change in an industry that eliminates your job or makes it less interesting. Other times, it is a proactive decision to seek out new perspectives. One way that is becoming more common is to "zoom out" in order to see new opportunities via time away from work. Consider Stefan Sagmeister, who runs his own marketing company in New York City and who has become famous for his unique take on traditional learning and work life. We spend twenty-five years of our lives learning, forty years working, with fifteen years left for retirement. His idea is to cut five years of retirement and intersperse them throughout the working years. Every decade, give or take, he takes a year off to maximize that time and invest in creativity, coming back with new ideas for his business and life.[6]

Elaine Cheung is a CFO who has changed industries and gone from being a music executive to working in phar-

---

6 Sagmeister, S. (2009). *The Power of Time Off* [Video]. Retrieved September 29, 2018 from https://www.ted.com/talks/stefan_sagmeister_the_power_of_time_off.

maceuticals and then retail, and along the way, adapted her approach to transitions within her career.

Her first "reinvention sabbatical" came after a restructuring. She felt very vulnerable but had enough time away to realize her skills could be applied more broadly, and then confidently moved into a completely new industry. The trouble was, she realized in retrospect, she hadn't really maximized her time off for the next stage in her career. Roughly a decade later, corporate restructuring triggered another sabbatical. Despite being the bread winner with three children under three years of age, she decided to turn this unfortunate situation into a positive experience. With a goal to explore whether she could combine meaningful purpose within work and career, she leveraged her experience and seniority to volunteer for an NGO called Community Business that works with large companies, where she focused on women on boards. This was an opportunity for her to meet people in the community, broaden her network, and advocate for women in leadership. It was very important to her, because when she dug into her values and contributions beyond her job, she realized she could have an impact. She wanted to be a role model, in a position to impact women coming up the pipeline. She could teach them about leadership and how to be a boss. On the networking side, it was extremely fortuitous, and she got her next job through those contacts, as well as several board seats, including on the audit committee of United Nations' World Food Programme, based in Rome. She's now a CFO for an aquaculture company, a spinoff from the owners of her old company whose restructuring triggered her first ever sabbatical. She is currently investing in her public speaking skills to take her advocacy to the next level.

There are few leaders doing what Elaine accomplished. She made a conscientious choice to learn something new, network strategically, and fulfill her broader value of giving back by being a role model and speaking about her journey.

KEYS TO SUCCESSFUL REINVENTION

Reinvention is about building on past success and understanding your core skills and attributes. Interestingly, when I coach board members, the same challenges exist as they transition from being, say, a CEO with very linear accomplishments to looking at the whole of their experience more broadly. I encourage them to look at their activities outside of corporate roles and responsibilities for clues as to what they can contribute to a board and examples of ways they can work with others to add value.

It can be a difficult transition to make, but there are lots of helpful, free tools available to help you gather data about your assets and purpose, such as the VIA Institute's Character Analysis, Gallup's CliftonStrengths assessment, and Imperative's Purpose Assessment. I will go over these resources in the action steps at the end of this chapter. In addition to identifying your assets and purpose, introspection will help you to uncover certain skills and enable you to build on past success. Following your interests is a great place to start.

SIDE HUSTLES, SLASHERS, AND SECOND ACTS

Steve Stine was always clear on the strength of his network. Over thirty years and while evolving his career from journalism to management consulting to business advisory, he developed and tended to relationships across the region. When he moved into the executive search business, joining Heidrick & Struggles in 2008, he had a ready-made network at his fingertips. He has also always been passionate about storytelling. To feed that curiosity, in his spare time he studied for a master's degree in mythology from the Pacifica Graduate Institute in California. Steve followed his offbeat tendencies as head of his firm's Asian region by negotiating to live in Bali because he wanted his daughters to attend the Green School, an alternative school focused on experiential learning. Stine managed his workload by piling up a ton of frequent flyer miles, visiting clients and staff in different countries and around the world.

His job and title put him in contact with a rich variety of

Asian experts and insiders. Blending an appreciation for "story" with the tale of Asia in transition, he launched what is today Asia's largest business-focused podcast, *Inside Asia*. He did this both as a creative outlet but also to enhance and enrich the quality of his network. His storytelling passion makes him very good at it. Meanwhile, the podcast nourishes and supports his interest in grooming his leadership advisory and coaching skills, as he reaches out to people to join him in conversations. This deepens their relationships to much greater degrees than the traditional transactional nature we're used to. In fact, his podcast has been so successful, he is thinking about how he can build or partner to grow a new and independent media brand and how it might lead to a completely new reinvention.[7]

Similar to the side project is the "slash life," where you may have multiple projects or career tracks simultaneously. This movement is based on a book by Marci Alboher, called *One Person/Multiple Careers: A New Model for Work/Life Success*.[8] Once the purview of the waiter/actor or receptionist/writer, it is often to combine paying work and creative or more purpose-driven work. This is now morphing into the professional world with violin-maker/psychologist, dentist/NGO leader, pro-athlete/investor or CFO Company A/CFO Company B becom-

7 Steve Stine (side projects), interviewed by Diana Wu David of Future Proof, September 27, 2018.

8 Marci Alboher, *One Person/Multiple Careers: A New Model for Work/Life Success* (New York: Business Plus, 2007).

ing more common. In the Philippines, there is an entire movement called "Slashers": people who focus energy on interests outside their traditional work. They might work as creative directors at an advertising agency then create jewelry on the side to sell on Instagram, using that money to travel (and putting the photos of their travel on Instagram!). As you build up your skills in a new area while continuing your existing role, the time pressure can be intense, especially if everything gets busy at once but the opportunity to be creative and fulfilled is worth it. If it seems daunting, a second act, or a sort of career serial monogamy, may be more your style. Ex-banker Agnes K Y Tai is another problem solver, always open to a pivot, who is pursuing a major shift in her work. While she has spent her entire life in finance, she has, in fact, been an entrepreneur without necessarily calling herself that. She told me about exploring new financial products and new markets, and about building companies, and she certainly had the courage to reinvent herself multiple times as the markets shifted and new opportunities arose.

Agnes has recently passed her PhD qualifying exam, following up on one of her ultimate dreams. After fulfilling various functional roles, she decided to get a degree focused on sustainable investing, incorporating environmental, social, and governance (ESG) factors in risk-rewards analysis. ESG is a very prominent trend as a way to focus investment on activities that are good for people and the planet. What she found was, that after forty years spent solving problems, she was in a very different environment, in a culture focused more on theory than practical solutions.

Agnes had a hypothesis about how this could work, but suddenly found that rather than applying an evidence-based approach, she would have to learn a new method of testing against original theories, with a historical perspective, and carry that forward. She's soldiering through but in a completely different work environment. Same industry, new environment; always an opportunity to learn in ways we don't expect.[9]

Reinvention can be challenging. It's useful to have stepping stones to new careers by developing hobbies and following curiosity as you go along.

MAXIMIZING TRANSITIONS

More people are taking time, or even family leave, to maximize investing in themselves and their curiosity, career focus and reflection, or to network in their field in totally new ways. Many learning opportunities, from iTunes University, to Udemy, to Coursera make it easy to invest in new skills, and almost all the major and minor universities offer classes online. Business schools across the world

9 Agnes Tai (second acts), interviewed by Diana Wu David of Future Proof, October 14, 2018.

have executive programs where you can spend a week or two learning something new. The importance of maximizing transitions will continue to increase because it's something that we will all go through. We rarely spend forty years in one company anymore, and we must learn how to adapt in ways that will help us in future work.

Everyone has transitions in life, and current work and learning trends may now allow people to get the most out of new directions. In *The 100 Year Life*, the authors predict that our lives will see many breaks for reskilling, work-life balance, or just broadening our horizons.[10] People are increasingly taking sabbaticals between jobs—a standard in academia or journalism that's now showing up in the corporate realm. Companies such as Intel, Deloitte, and Bain & Company allow employees sabbaticals to work on passion projects or professional development.[11] Today, some companies set aside time for people to do everything from working on interesting new projects to unlimited vacation days, where employees can structure their time to have a month off in the middle of a work year. Workers can take time away to recharge, bounce back from burnout, or help juggle conflicting priorities. People take time off to help a loved one, volunteer in a local soup kitchen, bicycle around Europe, or work on their yoga training.

---

10 Gratton and Scott, *The 100-Year Life.*

11 Glassdoor Team, "14 Companies Offering Sabbaticals & Hiring Now," *Glassdoor.com*, August 10, 2018, accessed September 29, 2018, https://www.glassdoor.com/blog/42136-2.

My friend, Mohammed Sam Soushi, had always wanted to walk across the Camino de Santiago, but he was unsure how to ask for three weeks off at his new job, even though he was already a valued employee. He was surprised to find that his firm was happy to comply. No one wants to work all their lives and then finally have time to walk for three weeks when they're seventy-five. They want enriching experiences and taking time away from work to have them is increasingly considered something that *adds* to your work as opposed to detracting from it.

In some cases, transitions won't have a natural end. Fabian Pfortmüller decided to document his transition from Holstee, a startup company, to whatever was next without knowing what *was* next. Within a year, he developed some fantastic ideas for maximizing transitions and discovered *that* was his new career. He saw that more and more people were thinking about transition and reinvention, and he started a company in part to help them.[12] Fabian now has an active Facebook community filled with people in all phases of life who are keen to learn how to transition in their careers. This was my experience as well, as I found that I enjoyed a portfolio life with maximum flexibility, and others were interested to know how to enjoy the same.

12 Fabian Pfortmüller, "Gather, don't train" – notes from meeting Peter Block," *Together*, August 10, 2018, accessed September 29, 2018, http://together.is/notes-from-meeting-peter-block.

EXERCISES AND ACTION STEPS

KNOW YOUR ASSETS, STRENGTHS, VALUES, AND PURPOSE

Many helpful and free resources are available online to help ground you. Here are some of my favorites:

- VIA Character Survey is an assessment developed in cooperation with Dr. Martin Seligman, the "father of positive psychology," which lists twenty-four character traits that can guide you to find work that is fulfilling: https://www.viacharacter.org/survey/account/register
- StrengthsFinder is an assessment that will allow you to discover what you naturally do best: https://www.gallupstrengthscenter.com/home/en-us/strengthsfinder
- Imperative Purpose assessment shows you what your key drivers are to find purpose at work and generates a sentence that encapsulates it (very handy when people ask you what your purpose in life is and you don't have an answer!). They also do this for teams and larger groups: https://imperative.com/

INVENT MODEL: GETTING YOU FROM HERE TO THERE

- Simon Kozlowski is a South-Africa-based reinvention coach who helps people around the world on their personal journeys of reinvention. His INVENT model is a simple, agile, customizable framework: The "I" in INVENT stands for immediate reality, "N" is for the new reality, "V" is for values, "E" is evolution, "N" references new thinking and behavior, and "T" is for test and improve. Maximizing transitions (what to do and how to do it): http://reinventioncoach.co.za
- Watch Stefan Sagmeister's excellent TED talk on *The Power of Time Off* which details his theory and experience on taking time off to refresh and reinvent: https://www.ted.com/talks/stefan_sagmeister_the_power_of_time_off
- Make a list of all the things you might like to do if you had three months, six months, or nine months off. This could become a fantastic fallback list for you, and one that most people only make six months before retirement.
- Consider making plans to take time off to pursue one of your sabbatical ideas. If you can't afford an extended break, can any of your ideas be cut into smaller pieces and done over time—say, one week every quarter?

YOUR SIDE HUSTLES, SLASH PROJECTS, AND SECOND ACTS

- List all of the side projects you have considered over the years.
- Pick one.
- What progress can you make on this project, or what can you do to learn what you need in order to pursue it further? For example, to launch a podcast requires technical skills in online recording and editing. Sailing around the world solo requires...probably a lot of therapy!
- Once you have a goal in mind, schedule time, locate resources, and take action to make it happen. For example, seek out a person who's already done what you want to do and ask them how they started and how they got there. You may offer to take them out for lunch to have this conversation, or if they're short on time, they may prefer a quick phone or email conversation. Then, take action. For my children's book, I met with an illustrator every Saturday from 9 to 10 a.m. for three months, which helped to keep me moving forward toward my goal.

Visit my website www.dianawudavid.com/futureproofinsider for more information, worksheets, and resources.

CHAPTER 5

COLLABORATE

In the long history of humankind (and animal kind, too) those who learned to collaborate and improvise most effectively have prevailed.

—CHARLES DARWIN

Today's world of work requires us to leave the competitive, "silo" mindset of most large corporations and bureaucracies behind and embrace the challenges and opportunities of working collaboratively and virtually. Collaboration, including intercultural competence, virtual connection, and personal awareness, is one of the most important superpowers we can develop. Technological changes, global communications, and the scale and the complexity of the issues we collectively face make it likely that collaboration will become even more crucial in the future.

Many companies have already caught on to the opportunity to work with outside partners or sources, hire the best talent from anywhere on the globe, *and* allow them flexible work options. For example, during my tenure at Pearson, we had a catalyst program to source issues across all departments and countries, and to post them for collaboration with outside startups. It brought staff together across departments and geographies to address problems and draw on outside talent; if the pilot was successful, the team would employ the project at scale.

Companies are offering flexible schedules and hours so that staff can work when and where they are most productive. Web-services company Automattic has hundreds of full-time staff working in twenty-nine countries—all working from home as a "distributed company." Isabella Wren, the fashion label set up by former investment banker Sarah Chessis, operates with an assistant and a group of freelancers for everything from PR to graphic design and photo shoots. Co-working spaces that allow you or a team to work around the world—a previously preposterous idea, given the cost of offices and set up—are becoming commonplace. Global Bank, HSBC, took several hundred spaces in WeWork Hong Kong to make space as they built up their digital team, and Dell, GE, Microsoft, and Deutsche Bank all use the co-working spaces for added flexibility.[1]

1 Uptin Saiidi, "Coworking Spaces Aren't Just for Entrepreneurs Anymore," *CNBC.com*, September 1, 2017, accessed September 29, 2018, https://www.cnbc.com/2017/09/01/coworking-spaces-arent-just-for-entrepreneurs-anymore.html.

This shift toward fluid networks can be difficult for people who have trained for traditional business careers, especially coming from years or decades of hierarchies geared toward optimal efficiency. Closed teams and rigid processes are good for delivering what already exists, but those methods don't generate new ideas, allow for quick responses when new threats loom, or capitalize on opportunities. As *Financial Times* editor Gillian Tett notes in her book, *The Silo Effect*, this division of labor yields efficacy but also tunnel vision, corporate infighting, and bureaucratic sloth.[2]

There is a prevailing sense that we can no longer rely on what was effective in the old days. On a professional *and* a personal level, most people are defined and limited by the scope of their job title. If we want to collaborate, it can be difficult to even imagine what we might offer outside of a specific identity as an engineer, or marketing or human resources professional. "In the Gig Economy, we can simply remove the rigid framework of a *job* and instead talk about how to encourage an economy of *good work*, no matter how it is organized and structured,"[3] says the doyen of the Gig Economy, the woman who literally wrote the book, *Gig Economy*, Diane Mulcahy. Beyond the confines of our corporate role, how do we gain the

2 Gillian Tett, *The Silo Effect: The Peril of Expertise and the Promise of Breaking Down Barriers* (New York: Simon & Schuster, 2015).

3 Diane Mulcahy, *The Gig Economy: The Complete Guide to Getting Better Work, Taking More Time Off, and Financing the Life You Want* (New York: AMACOM, 2016).

confidence to color beyond the lines or play well with others outside of our own sandbox?

PLAYING WELL WITH OTHERS

"That's not my job."

Have you ever entered a mall and stuck your head into the watch store to ask directions to the Starbucks? Have you called your local airline/cable guy/newspaper for help and been passed between people or asked to dial another number to get your problem solved?

Now think about the person who answered your call and found a solution despite it not being their job. You were delighted and surprised, weren't you? It's definitely not business as usual for them to go out of their way and find the right person to make sure you are happy.

We are taught to "play well with others," but working beyond your specific realm of expertise or obligation is not a given. In the not-so-distant past, "minding your own business" was considered an asset. Hierarchies were clear and narrowly defined. We could start off on a predetermined track decided as early as in our teens and, depending on the industry, climb the career ladder with virtual blinders on. No one had to talk to each other.

As a consultant in my twenties, I recall we were paid handsomely in part because of the failure of departments to work together. When we looked for solutions to a company's problems, we proceeded by interviewing people from across the company. Unsurprisingly, the best ideas and solutions often came from the staff themselves. I didn't quite understand why they needed to pay $400 an hour to hire someone as unfamiliar with their business as I was to collate their answers into a PowerPoint document, when the solution resided within the company's own ranks. Wouldn't it be less expensive to take all of their staff to the Bahamas for a weekend? Older and wiser, I appreciate the power of an outsider with time and perspective to collect and collate internal wisdom but still believe too little is spent gathering staff to work on the company as a whole.

This is evolving, and companies are moving away from bringing in consultants to tell them what they already know or would know if only they asked their own people. Now, specialists are brought in to help define problems and then create the capacity internally for teams to collaborate and perform. Specialist consultants can be brought on for specific expertise. Corporations commonly call in freelancers with specialized skills or bring in outside consultants to see challenges in a new light or generate ideas. Mature companies like GE engage the wisdom of the crowd by testing new products on Kickstarter to determine demand.[4] New technology such as LinkedIn or Asana enables the formation of new kinds of groups for connecting or sharing information and projects.

This requires senior leaders to change from an executive mindset to a collaborative mindset. Joseph Tcheng, Chairman of the Board at Clear Media Limited, described his surprise to me when he went from a CEO role to board director as a challenge, and opportunity, to transition from an alpha leader role to one of coaching and collaboration.[5]

Not every executive, accustomed to being rewarded for making decisions, is able to make the move quite as gracefully.

This requires a mindset shift and skills in recruiting key people to work with, having a sense of your own personal user's manual, and facilitating a team to succeed.

HACKING COLLABORATION

You can't have Google-like knowledge about everything,

4 Jeremy Kaplan, "Nugget Ice is Just the Tip of the Chewable Iceberg for GE's Crazed FirstBuild Labs," *Digital Trends*, July 24, 2015, accessed September 29, 2018, https://www.digitaltrends.com/features/firstbuild-nugget-icemaker.

5 Diana Wu David, "Chairing a Turnaround in China," *LinkedIn*, October 21, 2016, accessed October 28, 2018, https://www.linkedin.com/pulse/chairing-turnaround-china-diana-wu-david.

so you need to put together the pieces, and people, necessary to build something exceptional or solve a big problem. You can immediately work toward becoming a better collaborator by consciously widening your network. This goes beyond putting on a "Hi, my name is" badge, and making the effort to meet new people. Think about your network differently; map it out and identify potential partners across the community, including the people you speak to every day at the coffee shop, the people you work with, or old classmates. In the same way a good manager always keeps track of people she wants to hire, you can keep tabs on people you would one day like to work with on a project.

Social media theorist Clay Shirky has prophesied closed groups and companies will have to give way to much looser networks where small contributors have bigger roles and fluid cooperation replaces rigid planning.[6] Some company programs, such as Facebook's cross-team boot camps and the Cleveland Clinic's institute systems, are already doing this. Other workplaces would benefit greatly from a shift to open teams. This is sometimes done in the form of a *hackathon*—a short sprint where everyone gets together to try to solve a specific problem in a day or two.

---

6 Shirky, C. Gilbert, D. (2005). *Institutions vs. Collaboration* [Video]. Retrieved September 29, 2018 from https://www.ted.com/talks/clay_shirky_on_institutions_versus_collaboration.

Hackathons are common in the world of software, and the concept is now being applied in other ways and other industries. To try this experiment, gather a team of people who can collaborate on designing a solution around a problem you'd like to solve. Opportunities and results from people who have done this include sharing resources, sharing team members, and improving client care.

Brian Tang was able to bring together conservative legal and compliance professionals and tech software developers to create Hong Kong's first LegalTech and RegTech Hackathon, where the top Hong Kong team won at the Global Legal Hackathon finals in New York. I asked him how he found people with whom to collaborate. He replied, "Having been immersed in both the legal and regulatory, and then the startup communities, I would like to think that people know me as a doer, and not just a talker. We are trying to bridge different worlds and trying to do things that have not been done before, which may or may not work. I have been fortunate to have found fellow travelers with enough trust in me to join in this journey."[7]

The old version of networking with everyone meeting at the golf club has exploded into so many different levels. It's easier than ever to meet people around a passion and find out, in fact, that's the person you need for your next

7 Brian Tang, March 5, 2018.

project. This is a common scenario at marquee events like TED, Summit Series, or Mindvalley events quickly becoming the next generation of think-do tanks. The connections people make often evolve into collaborative projects. The United Nations has even co-opted this new connectivity to bring the best minds together to make headway on ameliorating global problems such as climate change and poverty, developing the UN Sustainable Development Goals in order to align and facilitate problem solving. As Ban Ki-Moon, former Secretary-General of the United Nations said, "We need to build a collaborative platform to achieve the full promise of the Sustainable Development Goals. We want to make it easy for everyone, everywhere to work together."[8]

THE RISE OF SEMI-PRIVATE NETWORKS

The rise of semi-private networks is helping to organize the people and companies we work with to create new value. Author and idea maven, Seth Godin, anticipates, "These entities will become ever more powerful as the economies of the firm begin to fade, replaced by the speed and resiliency of trusted groups."[9] A group of licensed doctors may belong to a platform to share certain patient

8 United Nations Secretary General, Ban Ki-Moon, remarks at First Anniversary of the Adoption of the 2030 Agenda for Sustainable Development, September 20, 2016.

9 Seth Godin, "Semi-public," *Seth's Blog*, September 19, 2018, accessed September 29, 2018, https://seths.blog/2018/09/semi-public.

information. Concerned parents and teachers might set up a discussion board for others working to help educate kids with special needs.

For example, Ellevate is a global professional network for women "leading the charge in changing the face of business." A group I belong to, Internet for Jobs (i4j.info), includes executives, NGOs, and entrepreneurs across the globe in a virtual, and occasionally in-person, conversation about a people-centered economy. Salesforce's Dreamforce, billed as one of the largest technology conferences in the world, makes connections across entire networks of clients and supply teams and encourages them to feel connected and part of the tribe.

These trusted groups can serve as either Special Ops teams or as Community Gardens. In the first instance, they are a network of people you trust by screening (licensed doctors) or mindset (people-centered work) from which you can assemble a crackerjack team to tackle a given project. These are often time-bound, results-driven, and specific to one goal. The ability of Médecins Sans Frontières (Doctors Without Borders) to gather a team of specialists to deliver emergency aid is one example.

If you want to cultivate your relationships over time for information sharing, building data sets, or content co-creation, you might consider a community garden. A community garden is the small plot in a neighborhood where neighbors come to enjoy the plants, cultivate flowers and vegetables, and participate in making their neighborhood a more enjoyable place for all. Define your space, have a good leader and facilitator, and invite others to come by regularly or contribute when they can. David Nordfors and Vint Cerf, cofounders of i4j, have led and facilitated this in their community, co-developing books and conferences. People can contribute as expertise or time allows. Relationships spin off into other projects. For example, education expert Donna Eiby has drawn upon people in the i4j community to help develop content for the Future Work Skills Academy (FWSA), a digital platform that brings together the world's leading contemporary thinkers and practitioners in the key skills identified by the Institute for the Future (IFTF).

Whatever way you find it useful to organize for your work, "Professional loyalty now flows 'horizontally' to and from your network rather than 'vertically' to your boss," Reid Hoffman paraphrases from Dan Pink.[10] In the future, it will be crucial to build up a network of trust, loyalty, and shared practice.

If you are someone who finds networking itself to be odious or you don't know where to start, consider joining

10 Reid Hoffman and Ben Casnocha, *The Start-up of You*, 6.

professional networks, past colleagues, school alumni, or business chambers. One trick I learned from entrepreneur and speaker David Goldsmith is to speak at a conference so that you don't have to introduce yourself; people will come up to you after your talk.

Finally, consider how you organize your network, be it on email, LinkedIn, with an Excel spreadsheet, or with a more robust contact management service like Salesforce, Nimble, or Contactually. These people are your future coworkers, clients, and collaborators.

YOUR PERSONAL USER'S MANUAL

With the increase in collaboration, the need to speed up the time it takes for teams to perform well together is key. You can help by letting people know how you like to work. I've discussed personal brand in previous chapters, but when you actually engage on projects there is another useful tool: the personal user's manual.

The personal user's manual is not a new concept; it's based on a 2008 *Business Week* article by Ben Dattner that resurfaced a few years ago.[11] In fact, it resurfaces every few years, and now holds additional currency with

11 Ben Dattner, "Forewarned is Forearmed: Give Your Staff a User's Manual—to You," *Business Week*, August 25, 2008, accessed September 29, 2018, https://dattnerconsulting.com/businessweek82508.pdf.

the advent of the Gig Economy and the need to work effectively with both freelance, company staff, and virtual teams.

The idea of a personal user's manual is surprisingly simple, yet powerfully effective. The manual reflects the style you have and how you like to work. When you get stressed, what is your reaction? Do you lash out and then forget about it, without holding a grudge? Do you need for someone to politely suggest you take a walk around the block? For instance, when I get stressed, I get very quiet and intense. I still want to work with the people around me but prefer that we make a specific time and space for that so that I can concentrate without interruption on the task I need to do. Otherwise, you are not likely to get a kind response.

Do you like to freestyle with your schedule or are you someone who needs more structure? I appreciate when someone sends an agenda prior to a meeting so we can maximize our time. Open-ended meetings with no clear agenda that go on for hours tend to annoy me. Of course, this isn't to say you should require a specific type of bottled water in your meeting room and be a prima donna about how you want to be treated. It's more about how people can best work with you, and for you to understand how others work, so you can make the most of those relationships.

Everyone in a group can create their own user's manual and post it on a company's internal website or Slack channel. I know of one startup that presents the CEO's user's manual in the interview process for new staff so that they see his good and bad sides and have a window into the culture of the company. His work style sets the tone for the entire organization. It's an indication of their culture and transparency.

TEAMSHIP: AN ALPHA ATHLETE PLAYBOOK

Once you have gotten your head around how to be a good partner and find others you can work with, it's important to develop your ability to succeed as a team. Who better to instruct you than Clive Woodward, the former coach of the England 2003 World Cup champion rugby team, who coined the term "teamship" to describe his take on the culture necessary to create a winning team. I had the pleasure to share the stage with Woodward at a global sales conference where he spoke about his journey from creating the perfect team to cultivating a culture of teamship that could be used across virtually any situation where great work is at stake.

As a coach, Woodward found he could tap into innovative methods to instill a sense of extraordinary teamwork in his players, including having them develop the playbook and set rules and norms for the team. His players decided everything from getting to practice on time to how they'd react when some were selected for big matches and others were not. Woodward urged his players to genuinely think about the emotional aspect of being on a team. Their dedication and group cohesion took them from being an average team to World Cup champs.

Woodward carried the Olympic torch at the 2008 Games and went on to head the British Olympic Association in preparation for the 2012 Olympics. Some of the teams were the best in their sport, while others were never expected to place. According to Olympic tradition, the teams moved into dorms, and despite his authority as a coach, Woodward quickly found that the athletes saw him merely as an administrator. Few of them paid him any attention as they focused on their individual or team accomplishments. Dorms were trashed, athletes violated team rules, and Woodward saw some of the players running around wearing gear from outlying sponsors.

This grated at him. He decided to go back to the basics he'd developed with his rugby players. Woodward knew that he had to get buy-in from all of the British Olympic teams, so he started speaking to them, in groups. He asked them about the problems they were facing and what was keeping them from their goals. With his unconventional approach, Woodward found some of the biggest problems were the easiest to solve. Moreover, the solution was often more effective and easier to implement at scale, rather than what teams could accomplish on their own. For example, he discovered some players fell sick and missed games. To ensure a match wasn't thrown due to stomach flu, he implemented a plan to sterilize all of the UK teams' bottles. He proved that creating norms for the teams through collaborative efforts benefited all of them.

Woodward also tapped into their sense of emotional pride by asking the athletes what image they wanted to project as Team Britain. He created a playbook across the teams for all they'd agreed to do, and because the ideas came from the group, not from him, he got a lot of buy-in. Britain's medal count increased, the athletes behaved well, sponsor problems went away, and they felt unity as true ambassadors of their country.

Considering the projects I've done in the past without established norms, it would have been tremendously helpful to have had a set of guidelines and norms around the frequency of communication, roles, and responsibilities. These are simple actions, but we almost never follow these steps on a project; we usually just dive in. This is good project management and good company management. Creating a space where people can do their best work is critical.

WORKING ACROSS SPACE, TIME, AND GENERATIONS

Imagine you've just launched your first collection for your new fashion label and the digital designer in the Ukraine that you found on Upwork has completed the website. A famous celebrity did a capsule collection for you so there is a launch coming up. An outsourced event company is planning it while your human virtual assistant in the Philippines is coordinating the invites. Meanwhile, your algorithmic assistant is emailing clients to schedule fittings for the new line.

This is the new face of work for many companies. With global connections ever more efficient, you can find extraordinary talent at often lower cost. The person who can develop the savvy to pull these diverse and distributed talents together is the linchpin, a person who figures out what to do when there's no rule book. "An individual who can walk into chaos and create order. Someone who can invent, connect, create, and make things happen."[12] Clive Woodward certainly demonstrated that.

How can you be a linchpin in the new world of work? In part, by understanding how to pull people together across space, time, cultural, and generational divides.

12 Seth Godin, *Linchpin: Are You Indispensable?* (New York: Penguin, 2010).

TRUST AND COMMUNICATION

The success factor of a virtual, global team comes down to trust and communication. For example, the board of a multi-lateral organization in Asia I have had the privilege to work with over the years has a diverse board comprised of regional or country representatives that would make your usual homogeneous corporate board green with envy. While working together to enhance their effectiveness, we discovered an amazing thing about the different aspects of trust. Despite their differences, most of the board had a background that lent them to define trust as transparency and directness. However, many of the staff in the executive ranks performed best when they had a sense of safety, which gave them the trust to try and fail (which incidentally mirrors the research on corporate technology innovation). They were not willing to be transparent until they felt the board had their best interests in mind.

Most staff also had a cultural predisposition towards indirect communication. The board did exercises around communication—direct, expressive, and indirect. For example, Americans are often seen as direct, and Asians are often assumed to be indirect, so as not to cause someone to lose face. I expected these stereotypes to play out during these exercises. However, when talking to this diverse group and asking them to go through some of the exercises, the board again showed up in almost exactly the same way—very direct and less expressive. It showed us that communication styles can change over time. They had all been in the same career to a large extent and that had shaped their communications and preferences. Even their attitudes of direct communication had shifted to realize direct is often good, if delivered in sensible ways. It was enlightening for them to realize that this norming did not extend to all members of the executive team.

Schneider Electric is an example of a company that's pushing to make collaboration happen across their organization. In their case, actual structural changes drove a change in trust and communications. Reviewing their organization's diversity, they found that 90 percent of top management was based at their Paris headquarters, and that 90 percent of those positions were held largely by French males. They looked at elements preventing them from being a more diverse organization and decided to establish three main hubs, in Hong Kong, Paris, and the US. This system gave more opportunity for people who had excelled in their own cultural setting to reach the top. They didn't have to move their families to Paris, which some people couldn't do or didn't want to do. This transformed the sense of advancement in the organization. One result is that they now have more women in higher positions. It was a nod from the very top of the company that they value contributions from everyone.[13]

13 Olivier Blum, 2nd Edition HeForShe conference, March 6, 2018.

Infiniti, the car company, also has this model, with a headquarters in Hong Kong, even though they're a Japanese company. They base manufacturing and design in Japan, and their biggest market is the US. They've created a global company that leverages benefits of each culture but collaborates for the best outcome.[14] These are all examples of companies who are going to more distributed teams across the globe in order to find the best talent, working productively and closer to the market.

A NOTE ON COLLABORATION ACROSS GENERATIONS

In keeping with this importance in attracting diverse, talented people to work together, we see the rise of intergenerational collaboration. In the film *The Intern*, a small fashion e-commerce company hires an older guy who just wants to work. He tries to retire but decides to take a shot at something totally different. You can see the generational factor at play: a company full of young people, and someone older shows up without any technology experience. The result is a charming culture clash, but the movie is a bell weather for work of the future.

Mentoring of senior execs has turned into reverse mentoring as young leaders bring their colleagues up to speed on new ways to work. There is a rise of new companies

14 Roland Krueger, American Chamber of Commerce Hong Kong luncheon, May 25, 2016.

that engage people interested in working in their later years. These companies allow the "elders of the tribe" to continue contributing their intelligence and experience without having to work full-time, and without the risk (to both sides) of a full commitment. There are also technology platforms that offer opportunities to do project work that fits better around offramps and onramps for parents or those caring for elderly relatives.

Global talent at all ages and stages, working part-time or flexible hours, often collaborating via some technologically sophisticated platform in constant change is set to be a new normal. It feels like someone has taken the nice puzzle we put together on the dining table and flipped it up in the air!

PUTTING THE PIECES BACK TOGETHER

Collaboration is the way of the future. You may not have consciously chosen a path into a large organization but may now be much more comfortable in the prescribed structure. Human beings like routine, and most of us have come up the ranks in a way—even through our education—that has rewarded us for managing within those systems. Perhaps you have a certain amount of trepidation about taking the leap into a less structured environment but knowing how to find the right partners will serve you well no matter what role you play.

Entrepreneurs may be the early adopters of collaboration because they were never particularly interested in the structure of a corporation to begin with, but anybody can get better at it. This will require learning people's differences and considering how to set up an environment that allows you to excel, outwit your competitive sets, solve important problems, progress, and learn.

Remember Brian Tang, who organized Hong Kong's first LegalTech and RegTech Hackathons? He was recently appointed the founding executive director for Hong Kong University's interdisciplinary Law, Innovation, Technology and Entrepreneurship (LITE) program. He is maybe one of the only people with the relationships to bring diverse people ranging from law firms, financial institutions, Fortune 1000 companies, startups, technologists, regulators, government officials, and academics all into the same room. Opportunities abound for those willing to authentically traverse different spheres.

EXERCISES AND ACTION STEPS

TRY A MINDSET SHIFT

- If you are not already familiar with a global, virtual, improvisational, open approach to working, think about how you might work outside of a corporate structure. Spend some time reading up on virtual teams and intercultural competency.
- Would you be interested in becoming part of a distributed company or virtual team? Do you have experience outside of a main job working with diverse teams? Often, these are the experiences identified as important in future project board work as it shows a collaborative, influencing style.

BUILD YOUR NETWORK

- Sign up for a professional association, alumni group, chamber, LinkedIn group, or another group that gathers people around an interest that relates to work you're doing or interested in doing.
- Review your network on LinkedIn or other social networks and consider what tribes you belong to. If you haven't already, sign up for groups on LinkedIn and consider commenting on other people's posts, and posting your own articles.
- A good way to remember what you're good at and

figure out where you might fit is to consider what you are able to do because of your years of experience: not two years as a corporate development person but someone who can review the China market for education opportunities and help other companies or startups navigate there.

- If you are stuck, go to a networking event and ask people about their professional challenges. Chances are you will hear a few for which you have immediate ideas, which makes you realize that you do have many talents and strengths.
- Commit to reaching out to at least one person a week with a call, email, or note to say hello or meet for coffee and share what you are working on or would like to work on.

DRAFT A PERSONAL USER'S MANUAL

Create a user's manual and share it with your team. Encourage them to do the same.

Think about some of the colleagues or bosses you have had (even though collaboration can be all peers, chances are we pay more attention to the needs of our superiors, so this may jog your memory better). What do you wish you knew about them before you started working with them? Answer the questions you wish you could have asked, but about your own work style.

Some ideas:

- How do you communicate? Email, text, call, in person? Formal, informal? How does it change for routine vs. important communications? How often do you want to meet in person?
- How do you make decisions? What kind of decisions are important for you to be involved in?
- When do you like people to approach you and how? Do you prefer working all together, riffing ideas off of each other or would you prefer we all go and do our parts and then come back to share?
- What time of day are you most productive (especially if you have to schedule global meetings early or late)?
- How do you want to engage with stakeholders? Do you prefer to work in a group or solo? Some people prefer to present their findings, while others prefer to work behind the scenes (are you the presenter or the guy with the spreadsheet?).
- What is your overall style?
- What do you value, and what is a deal breaker for you?

Once you've compiled it, you might ask some current or former colleagues to comment on how you are versus how you think you are. This document may change also depending on the situation or project, so don't consider it set in stone!

CULTIVATE TEAMSHIP SKILLS

Consider how you will set up the conditions for individual and team success. Some ideas to practice:

- Sit down with your collaborators and establish the common goal, team vision, and image you would like to project.
- Find the common goals and motivations and pain points in your team. Put those into the process to determine how best to work as a team. This is working *on* the business, as opposed to *in* the business.
- Codify this into a playbook that everyone can sign off on.
- Use your playbook as a solid onboarding process so that new people understand the team's rules and what's expected.

Visit my website www.dianawudavid.com/futureproofinsider for more information, worksheets, and resources.

CHAPTER 6

FIND FOCUS

The objective is to control your time—a non-renewable resource—and apply it where you have the highest leverage or enjoyment.[1]

—TIM FERRISS

Picture yourself in a small rowboat; the sun has set and darkness blankets the water stretching out to the horizon. The oars feel solid in your hand, and you feel a sense of accomplishment from the muscles you've built up and the callouses on your hands from the effort you've put in. It's a nice night out—not too hot—and a cool breeze ruffles your hair. The sound of the waves lapping the boat when you put the oars to rest is not unpleasant, but it makes you feel a little uneasy.

---

1 Tim Ferriss, "How I Built a #1-Ranked Podcast With 60M+ Downloads," *The Tim Ferriss Show*, April 11, 2016, accessed October 11, 2018, https://tim.blog/2016/04/11/tim-ferriss-podcast-business.

What if you are rowing in the wrong direction, getting further and further away from land? How do you find your way? What if your provisions run out? You want to feel like you are going somewhere that will be an interesting new landscape, or at least not hostile. You don't want to drift. Besides, you aren't particularly tired. You could put in more effort if you felt like you had some direction.

A small light sweeps the darkness, showing you the way and allowing you to navigate around the rocks ahead. You pick up the pace and row toward the lighthouse with a sense of purpose.

This may sound familiar as a metaphor for the stage in life where we find ourselves keen to continue our journey but unsure where to start or which direction to follow. We want a plan but feel like we don't have time to figure out what to do, or how to leverage our skills.

Don't spend too much energy trying to find your one true purpose. Philosopher, author, and founder of The School of Life, Alain de Botton, calls this "the vocation myth" that stems from prior religious doctrines where we hear the voice of God or perhaps the voice of accountancy calling us.[2] Most people never find an "ultimate calling" that

2 The School of Life and Alain de Botton (editor), *A Job to Love: A practical guide to finding fulfilling work by better understanding yourself* (London: The School of Life, 2018).

enlightens their life, and many of us feel embarrassed about it!

Instead, find a focus that can help you make better decisions as to whom you spend time with and what you spend your resources on. Consider the themes that come out of your strengths, values, assets, and who you want to serve. Set intentions about where you'd like to go and what you'd like to learn and take time to discover these things. Find the causes or problems that inspire you and find out what lifestyle, practices, and tools work for you. A well-lived life is one spent considering what is meaningful to you and finding ways to share it with the world in a sustainable way.

Seeing how much time we've likely spent learning things like the periodic table and the Pythagorean Theorem, don't we owe it to ourselves to spend at least a bit of time to consider, *Who am I? What is meaningful to me? What do I want to be remembered for? What gives me satisfaction and how can I incorporate that into my life? How best do I work and learn?*

WHAT'S YOUR LIGHTHOUSE?

Think of purpose as a lighthouse, or a North Star, to lead the way; a place of central focus. It could be a word, a question, or a commitment. It can be your focus for a year or longer. For some people, it is as specific as getting on a board in five years. For others, it is a dedication to make a personal impact on the younger generation at work. It allows us to remember what our priorities are when things get so busy, distracting, and stressful that we end up comparing things to each other, and solving our time management problems, rather than asking, "What do I really want to do?"

Let me give you an example from my own life. Several years ago, I knew I wanted to change the balance in my life to include those things most important to me versus the priorities of whatever job I was in. I wanted to become a better writer. Why? I love the written word and believe stories are a way to, as Gandhi put it, "be the change we wish to see in the world." Where facts fail, stories pull at the emotional heart strings and bring us into worlds different than our own. They allow leaders to paint an emotional future versus a thinking future to inspire people to action and meaning.

Stories have always been a big part of my life. As a child, I remember sitting around the campfire and listening to tall tales with my sibling. At the end of the school year, our big treat was going to the bookstore where we could pick out three books before going on summer vacation. This love of stories is a part of the essence of who I am. I don't think it's my one purpose in life to be a writer, but it's a direction I'd like to row toward.

In service to this, I decided to do a children's book as a side gig while I was working at my corporate job. At the time, there were very few baby books on the market that my children could relate to, so I solved the problem by creating *Hong Kong ABC*. This was, in retrospect, a pretty ingenious experiment because each letter had only a four-line rhyme attached to it, so I didn't actually have to write that much to create the finished product. It also allowed me to learn more about the marketing and publishing of books and network with a whole new world of writers and publishers.

After that experience, I needed a longer-term, broader vision. The intention of becoming a better storyteller emerged and allowed me to make decisions and prioritize interesting off-kilter ideas, like being trained by a former member of the Royal Academy of Dramatic Arts in London. It was an optional event, but I wanted to communicate and speak and reach people in better ways so attending this session fit in with my goals.

Actor-turned-communications-guru Trevor Penton videotaped many different scenarios and gave great feedback on engaging an audience. It was, of course, completely humiliating being taped and having to go over it in the presence of a professional actor. But it was incredibly effective training for telling a story and putting myself in the shoes of the listener in person, in a large group, or on television.

A similar opportunity had me unexpectedly (and unpreparedly) standing up at an open mic audition, after which the audience voted on moving me to the next round. It was not a comfortable experience; in fact, it was more like something you'd flee from at high speed. In the end, I was shocked to learn I was voted in and that led to the opportunity to do the TEDx talk in front of thousands of people that I told you about in the introduction—a very visible stage for someone who wants to be a better speaker. I put a lot of effort into that speech, but I never would have agreed to it if I hadn't known how important being a good storyteller was to me.

Recognizing the big themes, in our work and in our dreams, allows us to go beyond just our current job, which is important in an age of ambiguity. If we're rowing toward a job we hope to get in ten years, it's going to be gone by the time we get there. Broadening our mindset and incorporating personal and skills development allows us to realize more opportunities in the making. It allows us to have some structure and definition, but not be limited by it. And it might take you beyond "finding your Zen" to "finding your Venn." I'll talk more about finding your Venn in this chapter.

WIDEN YOUR LENS

To recognize your lighthouse, you can go back to your

strengths, values, and assets and see things through a wide lens. For me, learning and growth are big drivers. If a task or activity doesn't include these, I won't do it unless it's absolutely necessary. If I'm on a path with something I've done a million times before, I'll turn around or find another route.

I am sure we have all experienced being enticed by something that looked good but didn't align with our values. When we are restless at work, other companies approach us to do the exact same thing in a different setting, because they liked what we've done in the past. It's traditional recruiting—find someone who has done it successfully before and plug them into your organization to do the same thing. It's tempting but that doesn't motivate me; I'd rather do something completely new because I know it will be more sustainable in the long term and take me to a better place than spending two years doing the same thing that eventually nobody wants. If I'd gone that route, I wouldn't have spent any time investing in myself, upgrading my skills, or future-proofing my career.

Focus, but a soft one, is very important. Some people can think narrowly and cling to something with so much intensity that they miss oblique opportunities to find other ideas or collaborations that could dramatically enrich their lives. It's like being out in the wilderness tracking an elusive animal. Having that broad focus allows you to scan for good contributions that the market will value and to know when to zoom in on your target. This will allow you to do some "wayfinding," constantly assessing new critical skills or experiences that come up related to your areas of focus in an ever-shifting landscape.

FIND YOUR VENN

Remember the Venn diagram you learned about in school? The overlapping circles illustrate the similarities and relationships between groups. Similarities between those groups are represented in the overlapping portions of the circle—the sweet spot where all your various strengths, interests, assets, and aspirations meet. In his book *How to Fail at Almost Everything and Still Win Big*, Dilbert cartoonist Scott Adams calls this being the best "combo deal."[3] Instead of being in the top 1 percent in a field, aim to become very good (top 25 percent) at two or more things to find your focus. For Adams, his overlapping circles were cartoon drawing and his in-depth knowledge of corporate America and its foibles. Adams realized, "I'm a cartoonist and I'm a recovering corporate person. I could make money off of that."

We can no longer rely on somebody else telling us where to go. We need to find our own way. What combination

---

3 Scott Adams, *How to Fail at Almost Everything and Still Win Big: Kind of the Story of My Life* (New York: Portfolio/Penguin, 2013).

of disparate interests do you have that will allow you to make a contribution and become a category of one?

Let's look at some examples of people who have "found their Venn" in their own special niche. Learning about them may give you some ideas on the various paths you can take and how you might discover your own Venn. I'll provide links to online templates you can fill in to help you forge your own path in the resources at the end of this chapter.

Earlier in the book, I mentioned Mohammed Sam Shoushi, who was formerly in a government relations role at Google. When he realized he could better align his passion for mindfulness and conscious business with his skills, he was immediately inundated with lucrative offers to teach mindfulness and yoga. Taking a step back to reassess his skills and assets against his focus, he realized he could use his past experience working governmental systems and his interest in mindfulness to find where the circles overlap. From this, he had a vivid image in his mind of one day speaking in front of the United Nations. His vision was a culmination of his interests to help people individually, help people in corporate settings, and then to the highest calling of helping governments come together for a more peaceful world.

Once you find that interesting intersection, it can become

a lifelong mission. John Wood is the founder of Room to Read. In his book, *Leaving Microsoft to Change the World*, he talks about being an executive at Microsoft but with a deep sense of wanting to do something greater. He took a trekking holiday to Nepal, and while out on his adventures, a school headmaster showed him an empty library and 450 students who were eager to read. He then challenged Wood with a quote that would forever change his life: "Perhaps, sir, you will one day come back with books."[4] So began his journey to change the world one book and one child at a time by building libraries across the developing world, leading some to call him a "21st Century Andrew Carnegie."

Years later, he has raised over $500 million in capital commitments, has built a worldwide team of 1,600 people across over twenty countries, and launched education programs that have benefited more than 16 million children. He drastically moved the needle on literacy in the developing world, which is amazing in and of itself. However, what stands out the most is that he knows himself well, and like most great problem solvers and leaders, he has begun looking for additional challenges and opportunities.

---

4 John Wood, "Leaving Microsoft to Change the World: An Entrepreneur's Odyssey to Educate the World's Children," *Leaving Microsoft Book*, accessed October 28, 2018, http://www.leavingmicrosoftbook.com.

After hearing so many people ask how they could find purpose in their work, John again combined his exceptional leadership skills and passion for education to co-author a book titled *Purpose, Incorporated: Turning Cause into Your Competitive Advantage*. He's consulting on this topic, and that of leadership, with cutting-edge firms that include Facebook, Netflix, Nike, and Salesforce. Much like the Bill Gates philosophy of seeking "to unlock the possibility inside every individual,"[5] John is giving others room to grow beyond themselves and exploring ways to expand his work and to impact the world in new ways.

Lale Kasebi is another person who has found her sweet spot of focus. I met Lale when she was the global communications director of Li & Fung, a consumer product trading and sourcing company with over $13 billion in revenue, 17,000+ employees, and 15,000+ suppliers across the world. Established in 1906, Li & Fung is one of the oldest and largest companies in Hong Kong. Lale has always had a focus on innovation and was a champion for those initiatives within the firm. While bringing people in to collaborate with the company, her ambition to have more impact flourished. As she told me, "the company wanted to do things that transformed it and were unconventional. We moved fast and went right up to the edges of that. We knew we could do more. At forty—

---

5 Bill and Melinda Gates, "Who We Are," *Gates Foundation*, accessed October 10, 2018, https://www.gatesfoundation.org/Who-We-Are.

almost fifty—I just didn't have it in me to wait anymore. There were great examples of companies in action. I knew we could do more. I knew *I* could do more." When she thought about leaving to do something else, she found jobs aplenty but what she really wanted was a place where her full self could show up every day.

She returned to her values and thought, "I'm a leader, but I don't really care what company I'm in. My best experience was with my team, but I don't really need to lead a full-time team anymore." She began to think she could lead with ideas and create a movement without all the cumbersome infrastructure of office and staff and hierarchies. Lale then started *human-at.work*, a company that shows CEOs how they can initiate culture change, transformation, and trust. "It's about creating ideal conditions for humans and not just machines."[6]

In a world where most people are focused on computers replacing jobs, Lale used her innovation, leadership, and aspirations to focus on creating workplaces where people can truly realize their value as humans.

OK, SO WHERE'S THE INSTRUCTION BOOKLET?

My son loves to play with LEGOs. Whenever he opens a LEGO box, it's completely overwhelming to me to see all

6 Lale Kasebi (reinvention), interviewed by Diana Wu David of Future Proof, May 10, 2018.

those little blocks and how they're going to fit together. For him, it's perfect. Approaching the future of work is like that LEGO box. There are a lot of moving parts, and you have to figure out how they all fit together. Modern-day LEGO sets come with instructions, but master LEGO builders will tell you that to make something truly unique, you must throw away the instruction booklet. There are a few things you *can* do—instructions to follow—to begin defining your Venn.

DEFINE THE BIG THEMES

Deeply exploring your big themes offers opportunity to discover what's important without having to quit your job in frustration. It's an opportunity to reframe and re-craft your job to something more fulfilling. We live in an age of reinvention, inside of our job and out.

If, as you saw in the chapter on values, meaning is a key to a sustainable, happy life and work, you owe it to yourself to consider ways to think about work and shift your job to fit your interests. If you're an extrovert working at a library, you can lead library tours. If you're a teacher who wants to be a rock star, use your passion as a gateway to teach history and culture a la Jack Black in the movie, *School of Rock*. If you're the CEO of an insurance company and passionate about well-being, channel your knowledge and interests into your staff or even new products.

When I felt like my profit and loss responsibilities were becoming a bit stale, I asked myself, "What's getting me up in the morning?" Really, it was my team. I then spent a lot more time developing them and taking courses to be a better manager, helping people in the organization learn and grow. That refreshed everything for me and in turn led to greater profits. Though mostly a mindset shift, it made all the difference and better allowed me to bring my whole self to work. Social scientist Leah Weiss teaches a popular course on mindfulness and compassionate leadership at Stanford's Graduate School of Business. She says the path to productivity and success is to listen to the wisdom of our feelings for our sanity and for the sense of perspective we gain as leaders and as people.[7]

So take a deep breath and review your values, strengths, and purpose. There are great resources at the back of this chapter to get you started. The hard thing is the implementation. For example, I have always said my family is the most important thing to me, but I find it difficult to juggle family and a desire to contribute in my prime working years. Recently, I got a call from someone asking me to speak on the future of work at a conference in Singapore, and I really wanted to go. I hadn't been to Singapore in a while, and I knew it would be a good chance to catch up with all the people I know there. The event would

7 Leah Weiss, *How We Work: Live Your Purpose, Reclaim Your Sanity, and Embrace the Daily Grind* (New York: Harper Wave, 2018).

have been good for my work, too, and I was excited to go. When I got off the phone, my son said, "Mommy, are you going to be in Singapore on my birthday?"

Uh-oh. I love to have my cake and eat it, too, so I tried to convince the organizer that I would fly down for a quick appearance, but in the end, the logistics and my heart won out, and I didn't make the trip. I reminded myself that if family was really on the top of the pyramid, then I needed to make choices to reflect that.

I think it would be perfectly valid, at times, to do this exercise and put work on top, with family as the second priority. These are mutable priorities and they will change over time, if not day by day. By working hard, we can provide our family with a good role model and a roof over their head. This does not mean that family is less important than a job, but at certain times, depending on circumstances, the job does come first. Be honest with yourself.

DECISION MAKING

Big themes are useful but combine the broad inputs with some structure around how you will make decisions day-to-day. Set yourself up for success with a process. In her book, *The Art of Choosing*, Columbia Business School Professor, Sheena Iyengar, suggests we develop a sense of what the high quality quantitative and qualitative inputs are in our field.[8]

It's also helpful to consider consistent criteria or frameworks we might use. For example, Shane Parrish of The Knowledge Project has a framework that funnels his decisions into four buckets: reversible and inconsequential, reversible and consequential, irreversible and inconsequential, and irreversible and consequential.[9] This helps him focus on the important decisions and allows him to have a lighter touch on those that are less important, especially the consequential and reversable decisions that may take up time such as, "Should I get a desk at a co-working space or just work at home?" These can fall into experiments you can try and then proceed or cut, based on your experience. In the co-working space, you can go month to month and see how it goes without spending a great deal of time on whether it's perfect for you.

I asked super connector, Peter Williams, about his decision-making criteria. Peter is one of those "how does he do it?" people. On top of being a senior treasury executive at Citibank, he is a board member at Resolve, an NGO that helps refugees find their own voice, and at

---

8 Sheena Iyengar, *The Art of Choosing* (New York: Hachette, 2010).

9 Farnam Street Media, "The Decision Matrix: How to Prioritize What Matters," *FS.blog*, accessed October 10, 2018, https://fs.blog/2018/09/decision-matrix.

Music for Life International. He is Chair of the Chicago Booth Alumni group in Hong Kong, and don't get him started about skateboards or skiing! When I asked him what he uses to screen his activities, he said, "My criteria for engagement is, 'Could this lead to an adventure?' I like to put myself at risk of productive accidents." Over the years, he has developed a talent for being able to quickly assemble the people necessary to launch a company, event, movement, or community.

When Peter said yes to helping prepare speakers for TEDx, he spent time getting to know them, learning their stories, looking for opportunities to find shared interests and collaborate, and remaining alert to helping them advance the projects they care about. This led to opportunities for him to join the board of Music For Life International, attend a concert for the United Nations at Carnegie Hall in New York, then invite the conductor, George Mathew, to speak at a subsequent TEDx event in Hong Kong.

These productive accidents are what Peter feels will eventually help him figure out "how to help firms to create the conditions for continuous innovation, lifelong learning, and collaboration. At that point, 'what I do for fun' becomes 'what I do for work'...the creation of personal and professional adventure becomes my profession."[10]

---

10 Peter Williams (decision making), interviewed by Diana Wu David of Future Proof, Sept 12, 2018.

Peter has a laser-like focus on process and how he can quickly put together the people necessary to launch a company, event, or movement. In your own quest to define your Venn, do not overlook the benefits of process, or underestimate the potential for "productive accidents"—being willing to take risks with no promise of success.

Finally, backend the process by checking with a wise counsel of mentors. For example, when I asked Danny Khursigara, world-renowned coach and co-author with Jack Canfield of *Road to Success*, what his biggest challenge was in going from chief operations officer roles in banking to launching his coaching business, he said that the lack of structure and financial stability were things he had to learn to adapt to. He knew he didn't want to let financial anxieties distract from his vision, so he enlisted family and mentor support to ensure he was focused on where he could add long-term value.[11]

DESIGN YOUR LIFE AROUND YOU

People in positions of leadership within a company regularly create space for their teams to achieve great things on an individual basis. We must also do that for ourselves. One of the issues I hear with people who have taken a portfolio approach to work or have started their own

11 Danny Khursigara (mentors), interviewed by Diana Wu David of Future Proof, March 21, 2018.

company is that they may know what their big goals are, but they don't have enough structure. A good place to start is thinking of your perfect day and where you get your energy.

Consider what you want your days to look like. How you spend your days is how you spend your life. Does waking up to the sun and going for a walk in the morning mean it's a good day no matter how hard the work? Having a routine is especially important if you aren't required to go into an office. The most useful piece of advice I received on my first sabbatical was to schedule all my most important work before noon.

Design-thinkers Bill Burnett and Dave Evans at Stanford University Design Center found that one way to plan your day is by focusing on the energy you get from specific activities. Do team meetings inspire you but totally drain your energy? Consider some downtime after them. Public speaking gives me a tremendous amount of energy. If I'm researching and interviewing teams in the lead-up to facilitating a workshop, listening to their stories is fascinating, but I need quite a bit of down time to synthesize the information.[12] By tracking this across a week, their research shows, we can maintain a productive, not destructive, momentum in our work and life.

---

12 Bill Burnett and Dale Evans, *Designing Your Life: How to Build a Well-Lived, Joyful Life* (New York: Knopf, 2016).

LEAVE YOUR LEGACY

Instead of building from the ground up, the other possibility is to consider what life will look like at the end and work backward. Writing one's own obituary has long been a trope of personal development, in part because death serves to focus the mind and give us some perspective. The angst over the café running out of non-fat milk pales in comparison.

You can also consider a career eulogy. What do you want people to say at your retirement party? Were you the guy or gal who always exceeded target, the one who trained a generation of new thinkers, or were famous for bringing the entire office together over your fishbowl sangria? Think about what kinds of stories define you to date and what you want to be known for, professionally and personally.

Reverse engineering, it may be helpful to think of the *eulogy virtues*—characteristics like generosity, persistence, or integrity—you might want to include as aspirations. More than your "resume virtues," these are ultimately what matter most and define the kind of person you become.

In the next section, we'll look at setting yourself up for ongoing satisfaction and success by taking small, concrete steps that allow more control over a rapidly accelerating and distracting life. We'll harness ideas of innovation on a personal level and combine them with a timeless sense of meaning and purpose to reach the whole.

EXERCISES AND ACTION STEPS

VALUES

Take some index cards or Post-it notes and write down some of your priorities. They may be work, exercise, family, writing, aerobics, or visiting your mother—whatever you want. Form them into a pyramid, with the highest priority at the top. It's harder than it sounds. Most people talk about the most important part of their lives, but when it's all there in front of you, it's not easy to decide what goes on top.

For example, when I make a pyramid, I often talk about my family being the most important to me, but it's actually very difficult to put family at the top. How do I know for sure that family will always be the most important thing for me? As a good mother, I'm almost embarrassed to say that, but I realize how reality works.

TRACK YOUR ENERGY USE

This exercise, inspired by the Stanford Design Center, focuses on the energy gained from specific activities. List all the things you do during your day and determine how much energy they give you. A simple example is you might be very engaged with team meetings, but they totally drain your energy. Craft a day or a week to ensure you're doing things that engage you and spike your energy level.

WRITE YOUR EULOGY

What "eulogy virtues" do you want people to recognize you for? Not just what you bring to the marketplace but what you brought to life.

What kind of person do you want to be remembered as? Were you kind, courageous, and capable of deep connection? Develop a vocabulary for the character traits you want to develop. Write a tribute you wish someone would give at your retirement party or even funeral. Which of your eulogy virtues show up in it? What specific moments support those? Consider sharing these with a loved one.

Finally, be sure to visit my website www.dianawudavid.com/futureproofinsider for more information, worksheets, and resources.

PART III

MAXIMIZE: THE IMPACT OF YOUR ACTIONS

Success means having the courage, the determination, and the will to become the person you believe you were meant to be.

—GEORGE SHEEHAN

Part I set the scene for why things are changing. Part II was about activities you can do to help you on your way. Part III, *Maximize*, is about maximizing the impact of your actions—setting parameters for the long game of your career.

CHAPTER 7

REDEFINE SUCCESS

Success is liking yourself, liking what you do, and liking how you do it.

—MAYA ANGELOU, POET

The forces of competition and change that threaten business and industry also threaten individuals and their careers. If you don't stay ahead of the curve, you'll be blindsided by change. "Inaction is especially risky in a changing world that demands adaptation," says Reid Hoffman.[1]

If it's no longer likely or even possible to spend forty years at one company, staying put is also a risk. It's time to be smarter about risk by diversifying your options and redefining success in the context of life instead of a specific job. Now, "succeeding...doesn't mean finding a job. It

1 Reid Hoffman and Ben Casnocha, *The Start-up of You.*

means creating a more aligned, better balanced life, and finding satisfying work that helps achieve your vision of professional and personal success."[2] Don't settle for the life you've been given; prepare for the life you want.

RECONSIDERING THE IDEA OF SUCCESS

Now that you've learned skills to build upon for the future—experiment, reinvent, collaborate, focus—and adapted them to your own journey, it's time to see how to use them to redefine success on your terms. It's time to take the learning you have and pioneer new pathways to a life of trust, respect, balance, purpose, and joy. It's time to shed the external markers of success to make room for internal confidence. You can move to a place where you are perpetually expanding your contribution and progressively realizing the goals that will make up your life's work.

People have different measures of success, but there is a movement away from the traditional measures of money and power. Emma Sherrard Matthew, former Global CEO and now Executive Chairman of Quintessentially, a luxury lifestyle membership, has had a ringside seat watching her ultra-wealthy clients navigate their work and lives. She noticed that time was the greatest luxury

---

2 Diana Mulcahy, *The Gig Economy: The Complete Guide to Getting Better Work, Taking More Time Off, and Financing the Life You Want* (New York: AMACOM, 2016).

they were seeking. "Seeing all these incredible people, I noticed a trend. They have made an absolute fortune and they couldn't spend it because they have no time."[3] This resolution led her to craft her own portfolio career. This doyenne of luxury living now defines success by working with the people she likes, paying it forward by mentoring startups, and having time to spend with her young children. She has redefined success, for now, on her terms and laid the groundwork to be agile as she goes forward and as her priorities change.

Dan Wen Wei, a famous musician in China, was my next-door neighbor at the top of a fifth-floor walk-up back when we were starting our careers in New York City. Dan is now at the top of his game professionally, and likewise has found that time is wealth. After being a concert pianist in New York City, he returned to China where he is currently at a conservatory. There is a long waiting list for his teaching expertise, and he can pick and choose his students. In fact, he has to be choosy due to the high demand. He is often approached by celebrities or billionaires hoping to have him teach lessons to their children. His reply is, "I'll only work with those who want to do this professionally and full-time." Success for him is the opportunity to do what he loves, with people who share his passion and commitment.

---

3 Emma Sherrard Matthew (success) interviewed by Diana Wu David of Future Proof, September 10, 2018.

ROLE MODELS FOR THE NEXT GENERATION

One reason I felt compelled to write this book is because I feel that, although people are raising their kids differently than in the past, we are still in an era of time-worn expectations about success. I told my daughter recently that she didn't have to get good grades, that it's more important to learn in a way that fits her best, paying attention to her strengths. The way she makes friends, interacts with her teacher, and understands and manages expectations has equal impact.

She asked me, "What should I do in my life?"

"You're twelve," I replied. "It doesn't matter right now."

"What if I decide that the one thing I want to do in my life requires really good grades?"

I mumbled an anemic return argument but quickly realized she had the upper hand.

Kids today are very competitive. They're apprehensive about getting into good schools; they're in tutorial studies to gain every extra advantage. Ironically, it's much the same as the external pressure adults put on themselves. If all you've ever done is chase whatever seems to be right at the time without understanding your values and your talents, that method may get you a great first job but rarely is it the sole ingredient to a meaningful life.

Feeling like you're only able to succeed on your current path, unable to do anything beyond your existing industry, company, position, and skills, is a brittle definition of success. You can move away from prizing external validation, such as salary or titles, create new ways to evaluate success, and move toward valuing progress that reflects your unique values and priorities.

THE CHALLENGE OF FINDING PURPOSE

Many people are just hanging on. Others love the excitement of their jobs but know their role may have a limited shelf life, yet they have no conception of the alternative. Finding the next job is fairly straightforward; it's much harder to ask yourself—and figure out—what kind of life you want to have. As Natasha O'Brien, an HR services executive, laments, "There is so much information out there about success, but people still don't know who they really are."[4]

Why is this so difficult? Several factors contribute to this problem, one of which is the challenge of leaving one shore filled with society's ideas to go to an unknown place you can't yet see. Stanford's Bill Burnett calls this

4 Natasha O'Brien (success), interviewed by Diana Wu David of Future Proof, May 10, 2018.

"the society factory," with status, prestige, money, and power.[5] That is the ecosystem in which most of us work; it's a factory that makes us and subsequently molds us. To find new shores, you have to turn away from the one you're on and look to the horizon. Christopher Columbus said, "You can never cross the ocean unless you have the courage to lose sight of the shore." For most of us, it's not easy to let go of the shore and that lifeline we're used to.

One of my favorite philosophers, David Brooks, has a saying for this tendency to stick with what we know: "we're walking in shoes that are too small for us."[6] Tight shoes are the pits! Think about that for a minute. You know you have more potential, more audacity. It's a vivid image to think of yourself trying to fit yourself into something that just doesn't quite work, and you owe it to yourself to figure out something that *does* work.

HOW WILL YOU MEASURE YOUR LIFE?

At Clayton Christensen's fiftieth Harvard reunion, he realized that many of his classmates were enormously successful in their careers and proportionately unsuccessful at life. In fact, they were miserable at life because they had invested in their careers at the expense of every-

5 Bill Burnett and Dale Evans, *Designing Your Life.*

6 David Brooks, Danforth Dialogues, October 8, 2016.

thing else.[7] His book *How Will You Measure Your Life?* attempts to put that question to a wider audience. Is our own individual, professional success worth it? What is the cost?

In the beginning of the documentary, *The Diplomat*, director David Holbrooke makes the startling claim that only after his death did he realize his father, Richard Holbrooke, was a historical figure. The film is a fascinating look at the brilliant but divisive statesmen, ambassador Richard Holbrooke, made more poignant by the fact that his son manages to interweave the professional success Holbrooke had working on highly visible projects like negotiating peace in the Middle East, with the very personal story of a man largely absent from his family.[8] As he goes through the process of making the film, David realizes his father's sacrifices in pursuit of his passions, but realizes he is successful in his own right on his own terms, which are very different from his father's.

The late Holbrooke was a known figure around the office at my first job after college, working for Henry Kissinger. Kissinger, who has the noble distinction of having served as Secretary of State under President Nixon, and as my first boss (surely, a unique niche) put extraordinary effort into his work. Many people respect and revere him,

7 Clayton M. Christensen, *How Will You Measure Your Life?*

8 *The Diplomat*. (2015). [film] Directed by D. Holbrooke. Telluride: Giraffe Partners.

others dislike him, but either way, he has made his mark on history.

Perhaps that time was the "great man era" but you wouldn't have to look far to find modern equivalents, where people sacrifice everything to the altar of performance. In an era before cell phones, the entire staff carried pagers and used phone booths to dial in to the office if anything was needed. However, like Richard's son, David Holbrooke, while I have an appreciation for the dedication, I am not willing to make certain sacrifices to bathe in the powerful, political, and at times, celebrity limelight.

I didn't completely learn my lesson from working for Henry Kissinger. My work in consulting, which I spoke about in the introduction, was also 24/7. I spent every waking moment at my job. Even Sunday—my supposed day off—was spent doing laundry and expenses, and repacking for the next day. A car would appear every Monday morning to take me to the airport. I'd fly home Friday night, and if I was lucky and the flight was on time, I could catch dinner with a friend. Half the time, my flight was delayed, and my friends had already eaten and were ready to go home.

One of my friends said, "I just never know when you're at home, so I don't know if I should call." She eventually stopped calling altogether and that made me realize (if the thirty pounds I'd gained eating room service didn't) that I was living an untenable life. There are people who thrive on that kind of life, but I realized I wasn't one of them. Taking ownership of that realization helped me move forward toward a life I wanted.

When we talk about our lives now, it's easy to blame our 24/7 work life on the advent of technology and smartphones (or maybe, in the Kissinger example, the invention of the pager). Who hasn't waxed nostalgic from time to time about an earlier time when life seemed simpler?

I had a chance to test this question on the elder of a nomadic clan in Mongolia while I was horse trekking in the Altai mountains with the founders of the Nomadic School of Business, who were there studying nomadic mindsets. We were camping on the clan's land. They have managed the clarity of purpose, agility, and sustainability we now seek for ourselves; moving every season but able to keep their family together throughout generations. I wanted to know how technology was affecting that equation as cell phones, solar panels, and even TVs showed up in families across the area. The elder said, for them, technology was a blessing. Solar energy, for example, allows them to charge phones and maybe watch a movie at night or use a computer to sell their horses online. They can use cars instead of camels to move camp each season, and motorcycles to travel quickly between different villages, a task that used to take days. They welcome the tools and put them to good use but are not ruled by them. They remain respectful of the land, their rituals, and their purpose. They have a common identity and purpose, and their collective goal is to caretake the earth for generations to come.

MINIMUM VIABLE LIFESTYLE

Having a financially sustainable lifestyle gives you the flexibility to define success in broad terms. We reasonably think about work choices in the context of income. The more neglected side of the equation is cost. The more income we have, the more we invest in a lifestyle that gives us prestige among peers and the creature comforts that motivate us to keep working at maximum capacity. We build up expensive and demanding cost structures leading to an overhead that's often unsustainable in later life and rarely put into the context of the tradeoffs needed to pursue a broader definition of success. This doesn't need to hold us back. By planning ahead, we can ensure that we thrive in our lives as a whole, including career. We won't fall off a financial cliff, surprised by a health issue or redundancy, or caught out by a longer life and shorter terms in a more volatile world of work.

Extremely intelligent people who are totally capable can

become completely absorbed in the immediacy of their work. They're always on and always connected, and their careers are increasingly demanding. Just getting through the day can be exhausting. Instead of worrying about where the next job is coming from, ask yourself, "What kind of life do I want? Maybe what I have works for now, but is this what I want in ten years? What kind of meaning and impact do I want to have? What do I want my legacy to be? What kind of connections do I want to make? What purpose do I want to live by? What values do I want to live by?"

Studio executive Todd Miller is CEO of Celestial Entertainment and a veteran of the entertainment industry. He is a great planner and is perpetually mystified by how people don't plan well, financially or career-wise. He feels most executives don't think sufficiently far ahead and are only focused on what's next, either a promotion or the boss's job or a great job at another company. Most people don't take the time to think in terms of five or ten or twenty years, and to prepare for that.[9]

Years ago, faced with career burn-out, Todd took a sabbatical to bicycle across the United States and figure out his focus. He saw that many of his friends hated their jobs but were just hanging on by a thread because they had set

9 Todd Miller (minimum viable lifestyle), interviewed by Diana Wu David of Future Proof, May 3, 2018.

themselves up with an expensive lifestyle. This was his wake-up call to rethink his own next steps and reorient from planning for his next job to crafting the rest of his life. He realized that he did love his work and set about creating a plan to invest further in his career in a way that allowed him to do his work on his terms. He reviewed his costs and began to research investments that would allow him to be less reliant on just income, developed a retirement plan far in advance that included a great bungalow by the beach, and started developing the relationships and board seats that will ultimately provide interesting intellectual stimulation and ongoing work as he shifts into more of a portfolio career.

To think about setting up a minimum viable lifestyle or *MVL* to enable more choices in life, consider non-negotiables. I am lucky to be in a dual-income household, so we have more flexibility but lowering my income to write a book wouldn't feel right without first making sure my family was taken care of. If one day my children have their own ambitions and they cannot go to university because we can't afford it, I would feel like a failure as a parent. While, as Americans, we had the opportunity to set up college savings plans; these were accelerated to ensure each child had at least a year's schooling at a private school (no small feat!), and we will figure it out from there. We focused most of my income on savings and making a certain amount of headway toward retirement.

The second aspect of this is to have a crystal-clear idea of the worst-case scenario and plan of what you will do in that instance. Then you can conjure up some mitigating plans to ensure the worst does not come to pass or that you are prepared when it does. Business strategists incorporate it into scenario planning; author and self-experimenter Tim Ferris calls it "fear-setting" and says it's one of his most important tricks, while Silicon Valley pundit and founder of LinkedIn, Reid Hoffman, calls it "having a plan Z."[10] This is knowing in advance what job you might go for when your startup blows up and you need to get some cash to pay your credit card bills, or the sabbatical you take becomes a lot longer because your company restructures. It's the best worst option. It means imagining what life you have in that scenario, what apartment you live in, what food you put on the table, and how your life changes. That is the extreme Minimum Viable Lifestyle.

I've heard multiple versions of this. When I started a portfolio career I asked a colleague who had gone from being a hedge fund manager to a journalist what she missed the most about her former lifestyle. "Nice shoes," she said. Lifestyle maven Emma Sherrard Matthew mentioned that one of the hardest things is "giving up a big salary, working out the daily cashflow. I do have income

---

10 Tim Ferriss, "Fear Setting: The Most Valuable Exercise I Do Every Month," *The Tim Ferriss Show*, May 15, 2017, accessed October 11,2018, https://tim.blog/2017/05/15/fear-setting.

from being a chairman and from some of my advisory but much of it is angel investing, which will take three to five years to materialize. It's an adjustment."[11] Coach Danny Khursigara mentioned eliminating financial anxiety in order to be able to focus on the longer-term ability to add value. Todd has his beach house in Thailand to fall back on.

Most of this book is about keeping a job you have and beginning to build the skills necessary to move into a more flexible work that will carry you through the second half of life. However, even if you did stay in a well-paying, prestigious corporate job, you would be at risk of redundancy or mandatory retirement, so it is worth planning ahead.

WHAT DOES FUTURE-PROOF SUCCESS LOOK LIKE?

There's been a lot of discussion lately about what work will look like in an age of globalization and automation. I think we'll see people coming together, collaborating on joint experiments, and solving important problems. So what does a future-proof *life* look like?

A future-proof life is one that has considered how to mitigate the risk of accelerating change and disruption by

11 Emma Sherrard Matthew, 2018.

being prepared mentally, professionally, and financially. It is a life with a broad enough definition of success to honor the experiences, relationships, and opportunities you've achieved, not just milestones of achievement externally defined. It is always adapting and proactively seeking the next learning opportunity aligned with values and focus. Honoring yourself in more varied and creative ways contributes far more to your ultimate success. Hopefully through the activities, and also the many examples and stories throughout this book, there has been enough for you to imagine what a future-proof life looks like for you.

Reflecting back to my corporate lawyer friend, Jennifer: she didn't love every aspect of her job but thought a lot about her values and desire to help people. By doing so, she expanded into a role in thought leadership. This helped her win the top employment lawyer award in Asia, which she might not have been able to do without taking a close look at her passions. She followed her curiosity to a natural place where she leveraged her experience into something new, challenging, and exciting. Likewise, Lale Kesebi launched her strategy lab, *human-at.work*, to broaden what she did for one organization to other companies trying to build great businesses for humans.

Both redefined success, beyond just clocking in and out

every day, to reach further and be more ambitious about living their own visions of success.

AN ACTION PLAN FOR SUCCESS

I hope at this point that I've given you some ideas about your own future. My goal has been to show how certain minds thrive in uncertain times and give you the tools to do so as well. It's not easy to break from enduring habits, belief systems, and past prestige to explore and find new ways to grow personally and professionally. The greatest resistance we sometimes meet is ourselves. Yet we owe it to ourselves to create alternate opportunities and plunge in bravely past our own resistance to set a new course to new ideas of success and significance.

Remember that success can be broadly defined. A rigid definition exposes you to the risk of not realizing that the winds are shifting, and you might not be ready. The company you work for may no longer be around in the coming years, or the industry might be dramatically disrupted. With self-awareness and courage to act, you can prepare for those kinds of events and capitalize on the lack of structure to create one that best serves you.

Don't wait for success to come to you and don't think that once you have it, it's there forever. Think about where you are today, where your work is heading, and take calculated risks to get where you want to be. Most people reading a book like this are already in that frame of mind or they're nervous and not exactly sure how to move forward. Yet they have a lot of career capital and can become leaders in the new economy. To maximize your potential, it's vital to think, reflect, and shift your perspective. Many of us are already leaders of some sort, which makes us even more responsible to think and reimagine the future of work for ourselves and others. Get out there and challenge your ideas. Craft your own life and role model the possibilities of the future. It's time to act.

CHAPTER 8

REBALANCE YOUR PORTFOLIO

Enjoy the little things, for one day you might look back and realize they were the big things.[1]

—ROBERT BRAULT

Artists and writers have portfolios of their best work. Investors maintain diversified portfolios of financial investments. This chapter refers to your life portfolio, where and how you spend your time, energy, and resources. The idea is to consciously consider the risks, rewards, and time of life, and rebalance that portfolio by investing in future-proofing your career and factoring in life-long success.

1 Robert Brault, "Who Wrote Enjoy the Little Things...?" *The Robert Brault Reader*, June 4, 2018, accessed October 11, 2018, http://rbrault.blogspot.com/p/who-wrote-enjoy-little-things.html.

Recognizing this need to rebalance changed the way I spent my time. When my kids were born, I always said family was the most important thing—the top of my pyramid. Even so, I worked eighty-hour weeks and spent most of my spare time thinking about work. That lifestyle had worked a little better when I was young, had no partner, no kids, and no personal life, but it wasn't a great long-term option.

What would life would look like if we spent more time on what mattered most?

Asking myself that question was my starting point and revealed a huge imbalance. I said my family was most important, but I spent less than an hour a day with the kids, spread out over snapshot increments in the morning and then at night, getting them ready for bed, which was a grumpy affair. The people I really wanted to spend time with ended up with twenty rushed hours of me in a good week, while I gave eighty enthusiastic hours to my job. Forget about the hours I needed to maintain my basic health!

It was out of sync with my values and what I wanted in my life. Looking closely and honestly at what I was doing, I focused more on what I truly wanted. This experiment spurred me to reduce my work schedule from a regional role to a faculty program director that required less travel. I was amazed at what I found in my own town when I didn't leave it every other week: poetry readings, awesome new restaurants with my husband, and even strolling down the street without grumbling about how slow everyone moved. I invested more in the community via my board work and volunteering, preparing vulnerable youth for the future of work, and mentoring some amazing social entrepreneurs. It was a wonderful and terrifying experience, about the same immediate cost as my MBA but with far more learning in return.

FAMILY PRIORITIES REVISITED

Taking this approach toward work also allows you to gain some perspective around other priorities so you can make better decisions for yourself and your family. For example, around the time I made this dramatic career shift, my mother became sick.

During that time, I was scheduled to lead a workshop in Singapore. In the same week, I needed to meet with my brother and mother. I decided to ask someone else to go to the conference and was able to spend a great week in Arizona with my family. In the past, it would have been a road warrior itinerary of one day in each city and four days of travel. And for what? A bigger bonus or a better job title?

If she had gotten sick when I was working all those crazy

hours, I would have squeezed in brief visits. Instead, I took significant time off, making six Pacific Ocean crossings, including a few with our three kids in tow. Many people I know end up flying home to a family deathbed moment. We've lost touch with honoring life's fundamentals: birth, death, celebration, and sickness. I'm grateful for the chance to spend time with our extended family before it is too late.

My family at home needed me, too. My son came home from school in sour moods. He hated school and was anxious about everything. Prior to having the time, all I did was try to keep the wheels on the bus. It was always go, go, go, hurry up or we're going to be late. I finally started slowing down and truly listening and connecting with my kids. I realized that if I fully engaged with my team at work, I should be doing that at home, too. I spent time deliberately fitting life and work together, so I could be available for the people who needed me. I was already attending almost every school play and parent-teacher conference, but I needed to put the same effort into downtime with my family, being *with* them instead of checking off my attendance. I was doing things backwards. Now I've shown my kids that we have choices and, even when we choose to work hard, it's important to have that be an intentional choice. When I ask my children, they still say I still work too much, but they know how excited I am about the projects I am doing and actively participate in them as well.

Best of all, the experience benefitted our family in other ways. I asked my daughter what she thought about the change in our work-life balance and she said, "Mom, I learned that sometimes you have to take risks to do what's important to you." I couldn't have said it better.

AUDIT YOUR LIFE

Generally the word "audit" doesn't strike joy into many hearts. But one of the most rewarding methods for starting to rebuild and rebalance a life portfolio is by completing a life audit. Like a financial audit, this process shows you what you're accomplishing against what you think you're doing. It's simultaneously simple and illuminating.

It is helpful to separate the life audit into three distinct components:

1. Time audit
2. Trust audit
3. Financial audit

TIME AUDIT

If you look at your calendar and compare it against your values, life goals, and focus, does it add up? Take an hour to flip back through the last six or twelve months in your calendar and write down some of the chunky bits and what they do to help you align your life with what you would like to do. Does it feed your growth? Does it prioritize your health? Does it enhance learning in the area you've identified as a good pivot? Does it contribute to developing the values and virtues you want to project. Have a category called "other" and write down all those activities you do that *don't* enhance your life. Does it take up 20 percent of your life? Two percent? Who are you spending your time with, what projects do you spend time on, and how does that time line up with your priorities?

Review your calendar quarterly and ask, "What did I do this quarter, and did it work? Was it important to me? Did it line up with my priorities? What can I do daily, weekly, or monthly that makes next quarter look better?" I know there are productivity nuts (I wish I was one of them) who schedule their days to the minute. If you are one of them, this is likely too basic for you, but even great schedulers can lose sight of the bigger picture.

If there are areas you want to invest time in, schedule something discreet, like taking a course or taking on a project around a skill you want to learn or master. Remember that writing I wanted to get better at? I signed up for a critique group with the local writer's circle. It still seems unfair to subject the amazingly talented guys in my group to my writing, but they seem to be patient, provide great feedback, and I have a built-in incentive to put time in to creation and feedback.

Scheduling exercise is also important to the people I interviewed: resilient body, resilient mind. I structured my day by ensuring my most important priorities, including health, were accomplished by lunch. In early iterations of my time audits, I knew I wanted to get up early, write for thirty minutes, exercise, and spend time with my family. After that, I'd spend three hours crafting my work and then go spend time in face-to-face meetings later in the day. Knowing my personal priorities would be tended to first was very important and helped streamline different aspects of my life.

TRUST AUDIT

The trust audit is key for resilience and your network. Who do you trust deeply? Who are your 3 a.m. friends? Have you focused on creating intimacy and love in your life to support yourself?

Having a lot of friends who are a pleasure to hang out with is absolutely fantastic and often leads to new and interesting opportunities to collaborate and network. You don't need to be transparent and tell them everything about your life. You need a select few whom you can reach out to any time, confide in, and be vulnerable. Some people tell me, "Diana, you need to get back on the corporate track. I can't understand why you're ruining your life like this." Other people think my life is a complete joy and I have it made, barely working but still managing to launch projects, traveling the world teaching and consulting, and having time for family. The ones I spend the most time with are those who say, "If that's what you want to do, that's great. How can I help?" If I fail, those are the people who will encourage me to move past the obstacle and on to greater things, or they'll tell me I'm full of it and point out the risks so that I can better prepare. Having that trust circle and those relationships is important; it's something we don't always teach the next generation, and we should.

FINANCIAL AUDIT

Many books provide financial planning tips in detail and, as mentioned in the intro, this is not one of them. In fact, a friend of mine is writing one now, and he feels that money is the central issue. He maintains that only by taking money out of the equation can you make decisions on values and purpose. Perhaps he is right but a famous study from economist Alan B. Krueger and psychologist Daniel Kahneman shows that higher income rarely correlates with time spent on meaningful activities or increased happiness.[2]

---

2 Eric Quiñones, "Link Between Income and Happiness is Mainly an Illusion," *Princeton University*, June 29, 2006, accessed October 11, 2018, https://www.princeton.edu/news/2006/06/29/link-between-income-and-happiness-mainly-illusion.

It's important to know how much money you need to live your Minimum Viable Lifestyle. What does it look like now and what does it look like over the long run? Do you need to move to a different city? Does that work for your long-term plans (e.g. a house in Colorado fully paid off you can live in) or is it a short-term experiment (can I really live on the beach full time?). Can you forgo buying new clothes for a year, a decade? Will you send your kids to state-funded schools instead of private so you can pursue your art more? Are you ready for them to miss out on prestige for the opportunity to show them about making choices in life? Go through the entire household budget and long-term plans to see what you can strip out. You may be amazed by what you are spending money on that isn't strictly required. The advertising world does an excellent job connecting people's material wish list to their deepest Maslow's hierarchy of needs, but the result isn't always truly fulfilling.

Now consider the dreams and goals that have come up in your explorations. Write down as many as you can. Some of them will require money but many just require time. Understand the tradeoffs and get creative about putting the puzzle pieces together. Do you want to take a month off to go to art school or trek in Peru? Start to consider the non-material values you want to pursue and how to "buy" them by reducing in other areas or getting creative about your collaborations and projects. When lawyer Jennifer

Van Dale moved into thought leadership work, I asked her about other things she might do. She said, "I am very passionate about photography, but I don't want to monetize my passions. I want to set up my work so that I have time and resources to pursue them without money being an issue."[3] That is often a great way to improve the way you show up to your other work.

Finally, look at how much income you need to sustain your minimum needs; explore what is enough work or enough money for you. Rather than defaulting to a forty (or eighty) hour workweek, could you work two days a week? Work hard now and save art school for a sabbatical or redundancy? Start adding in the items from your dream list. Do you need to consider building up passive income via real estate, investments, or even a side hustle to create a side income to weather storms and create an alternate opportunity for experimentation? With the right tools and, more importantly, the right mindset, this can be a very pleasurable journey.

The leaders at Stanford Design Lab remind us that this is a never-ending project; you never finish designing your life.[4] We are always tinkering until something looks good for now, then adding to the picture with new experiences.

---

3 Jennifer Van Dale, 2018.

4 Bill Burnett and Dale Evans, *Designing Your Life*.

AFTERWORD

It's natural to yearn for permission to do what's right for yourself, but taking ownership of your desires to proactively create a professional and personal life that works for you takes both courage and effort.

EXPLORE AND EXPERIMENT

Explore your values and understand what makes up your bedrock. From there, you can experiment and learn new skills to see what kinds of ideas you can bring into your life. Small experiments quickly executed allow you to understand how to explore, gain feedback, and craft a future that fits your goals, not someone else's.

I like to think of collaborating and experimenting as similar to crossing an unsteady bridge you've never crossed before, unsure of what lies on the other side. You test one step and see how it feels, then take the next. Once you get the feel of the first, the rest aren't so intimidating.

COLLABORATE

Collaboration is a driving force in this process, and while it has been enabled and enhanced by technology, it doesn't necessarily replace human-to-human collaboration. With a better sense of awareness about global and virtual options, flexibility, and your own user's manual, you can effectively collaborate with people on new projects and maximize your impact.

REINVENT

With job tenures decreasing and our lives lengthening, we live in an age of reinvention. It has become a necessity rather than just a nice to have. You explore new interests and accumulate new skills to perpetually reinvent yourself. Your reinvention accelerates change in your life and work. This often isn't easy, and it can be scary to let go of things you think are important. Yet once you move on, reinvent, and evolve, you'll find yourself looking back and wondering why you didn't make the change sooner.

For people who have achieved a certain amount of success, it can feel like looking over the edge of a cliff. So many people achieve excellence in one area and are then afraid of tackling other areas because they fear they'll no longer be able to shine or be the star. They deprive themselves of becoming a broader, more valuable person even in their profession. However, as you learn to trust in yourself and your own creative process, you'll find yourself building your own bridge, one step at a time, across the chasm. You'll also find that you're not alone on the bridge, even when it sways in buffeting winds.

FOCUS

Focus changes over time, but taking time to craft the big themes, current priorities, and how you can live your life to align with them allows you to build on the past and adapt to the future. Start with a eulogy for your career and life and reverse engineer it to plan your weeks and days.

REDEFINE SUCCESS AND REBALANCE YOUR LIFE

Any wise life is aware of what success has cost. All these elements can encourage us to redefine success on our own terms. What is important? What will be your value legacy? There are so many ideas and options to consider as you redefine success and rebalance your life. You need to reflect on the risks, the rewards, the costs, and the benefits, but most importantly, the *possibilities.*

As you explore those options you'll arrive at a calm and

still place in yourself. You'll move from external to internal validation, working in the context of a great life, rather than trying to fit life around work. As you overcome fear and resistance, you'll find a strong internal compass.

FUTURE-PROOF YOUR LIFE

When I changed my life balance, I returned to Bronnie Ware's article—which is now a book—for inspiration, *The Top Five Regrets of the Dying*. Her regrets list is a great platform for a meaningful, agile, and fulfilling life. Here is what she found:

> "I wish I hadn't worked so hard...I wish I'd had the courage to live a life true to myself, not the life others expected of me...I wish I'd had the courage to express my feelings...I wish I had stayed in touch with my friends...I wish that I had let myself be happier."[1]

Investing in your own happiness, having authentic relationships, and expressing your feelings is ultimately a life without regret.

There has never been a better or more important time to do this. Jobs today are becoming more fluid, with people moving among teams and between fields far more often.

---

1 Bronnie Ware, "Regrets of the Dying," *BronnieWare.com*, accessed October 10, 2018, https://bronnieware.com/blog/regrets-of-the-dying.

Self-awareness is the new success and the only way to survive. Don't define yourself too narrowly. Learn to ground yourself at your core in the values of connection, commitment, and resiliency. It will help you see more clearly how your skills can take you much farther than your present position or job title.

Futurists, economists, and politicians tell us that robotics, automation, and artificial intelligence will not completely replace jobs but will drastically change them. Things are changing fast, but those who are adaptable and forward thinking will find a place to succeed and thrive in the new workplace.

PERMISSION GRANTED

People want permission to create their own path. They grow up with their parents, their friends, schools, and work, usually following a path that has already been laid. The winners in the future of work will be those who make their own roads.

When I go out and speak to companies, I'm surprised by how many people have the sense that they know what they want to do but don't feel they have permission to do it. They say: "I have an idea. I know what I want, but it just seems insurmountable. Are people even allowed to do that?" They've done everything right in their careers.

Now they want to do something different, and they're afraid that if they change, everybody will be mad or disappointed in them. Imagine what opportunities could be uncovered if we all had a bit more courage.

I hope that in some small way I can inspire you to begin to experiment. To me, personally, growth is all about trying new things.

Taking that first step always leads to change. If you're stuck in a particular way, make a small change, and see how it works, then build out to new practices and habits. Explore learning new skills and gaining new abilities. Reinvention doesn't occur suddenly; it's a process of evolution. Let me know how it goes.

I wrote this book because experience has shown me that now is the time to future-proof our lives and careers. My goal on these pages has been to pay it forward and build a future-proof community to help each other as we go into what promises to be a challenging time. Let's collectively move to assist others in finding their own paths forward to living life on their own terms and having a satisfying future.

Come join me at www.dianawudavid.com/futureproofinsider.

APPENDIX

Connect with me and others on www.dianawudavid.com/futureproofinsider, where you'll find more information to help you future-proof your career and life.

Exclusive content includes:

1. A free Future Proof self-assessment checklist, which can show you where you are doing well and where you may want to focus on improvements.
2. Downloadable exercises from each chapter.
3. An executive summary of Future Proof with key points summarized for you to share with others in your network.
4. Links to further reading and resources, blogs, websites, twitter feeds and more.

Look forward to connecting!

—DIANA WU DAVID

ACKNOWLEDGMENTS

There are many people who have been important and encouraging on the road to writing this book. At the risk of leaving someone out, I wish to acknowledge:

You, for your ambition to craft your own life and role model the possibilities of the future. It's never easy to forge your own path. I hope this book will be useful. Pay it forward, help someone else, make a movement, and form a future-proof community to help others.

Many comrades shaped my thinking and ideas about how to live life in the new economy. Some of them appear as stories or in quotes in the book. Many do not but have equally contributed to the conversation: Alex Crutchfield, Danny Khursigara, Eric Simm, Mohammed Sam Soushi, Todd Miller, Steve Stine, Anthony Willoughby, Josie Stoker, Jennifer Van Dale, Lale Kasebi, Stefanie Myers,

Nashua Gallagher, Kate Otto, Simon Kozlowski, Elaine Cheung, Brian Tang, Mark Piesanen, Leong Chung, Michelle Paisley, Shveitta Sharma, Natasha O'Brien, Peter Williams, Lori Granito, Laura Winwood, Elizabeth Loenborhn, Vicki Rothrock, Cathy Strittmatter, King-sze Yip, Tanya Wong, Canice Lam, Beatrice Remy, Michelle Lombard, Shalini Mahtani, Gita Sriram, Grace Clapham, Richard Claydon, Prassana Bhaskar, Jennie Orchard, Kate Otto, Agnes Tai, Priyanka Gothi, Julia McNamara, and Susan Bird.

Fellow future of work / future of education zealots: Donna Eiby, Heather McGowan, Jonathan Shell, Jane Horan, Hitendra Wadhwa, Jennifer Van Dale, Natalie Chan, Yat Sui, Anthony Davies, Mike Michalec, Annette Schoemmel, and Arnold Chan. Vint Cerf, David Nordfors, the internet4jobs crew, and the tedxwanchai community. You have all helped consider which ideas are worth spreading.

Financial Times colleagues and friends: Angela Mackay, Hannah Carmichael, Karen Cho, Anna Lam, Chris Moon, Ray Baker, Vincci Chung, Brian Schroeder, and Dr. Steven DeKrey.

Book Team: Julie Arends, Claire Winters, Susan Paul, Zach Obront, and Jesse Sussman.

My parents, Ronald David and Eloise Jensen, who raised

me to always question and strive to make an impact and who have embraced all of my harebrained adventures with equanimity and amusement. My brother, Sam David, who has always been my wise counsel.

Florence, Angel, and Lea for being my super family support system.

Finally, my family, the best investment I've ever made. Thank you, Alan, Emily, Alex, and James for being understanding about time away and missed bedtime stories so that I could write. I hope when you grow up you will be able to live life on your own terms.

ABOUT THE AUTHOR

DIANA WU DAVID is a strategist, innovator, entrepreneur, and the founder of Sarana Capital and Sarana Labs. Her companies transform how executives work and prepare companies to be more entrepreneurial, resilient and successful in the face of constant change, invest in edtech and HRtech, and support innovative education initiatives across public and private sectors. Her diverse, global career includes assisting Henry Kissinger and leading executive education initiatives for *Financial Times*. A superconnector of people and a sought-after speaker, Diana lives in Hong Kong with her husband and their three children.

CPSIA information can be obtained
at www.ICGtesting.com
Printed in the USA
LVHW112319290819
629477LV00001B/57/P